PERMISSION TO CREATE

PERMISSION TO CREATE

EMBRACE YOUR ART AND UNLEASH YOUR TRUE POTENTIAL!

NATE JONES

STORIES FROM A GRAMMY BALLOT ARTIST

NEW DEGREE PRESS

PERMISSION TO CREATE
Embrace Your Art and Unleash Your True Potential!

ISBN   978-1-63730-356-6   *Paperback*
        978-1-63730-357-3   *Kindle Ebook*
        978-1-63730-358-0   *Ebook*

This book is dedicated to my Uncle Marco and my Uncle Al, two great men who loved music almost as much as they loved their families.

CONTENTS

—

"If you want to find the secrets of the universe, think in terms of energy, frequency, and vibration."

—NIKOLA TESLA

"We are souls dressed up in sacred biochemical garments and our bodies are the instruments through which our souls play their music."

—ALBERT EINSTEIN

INTRODUCTION: GO BIG!

"Music is a higher revelation than all forms of wisdom and philosophy."

—LUDWIG VON BEETHOVEN

When I first picked up my childhood electric guitar back in 2012 at the age of nineteen, I had no idea that a mere seven years later I would be competing against Sir Paul McCartney for not one, but two GRAMMY awards.

I can vividly recall one warm summer evening in 2018 writing the words "GO BIG FOR EVERYONE" in all capital letters on my white board. I had just finished listening to *Big Magic* by Elizabeth Gilbert on audiobook. I was truly blown away by how much it moved me, how much it stirred the deep longing I always had to do something extraordinary with my life. The problem was I was good at many different things, but never great at any one thing. I enjoyed many things, but I had not yet cultivated a deep passion for any particular skill or activity or field. That is, until I found music.

A few days after writing those words on my whiteboard, my band Neapolitan decided to record our first album at a studio called Big Nice. I acknowledged to myself that it was a bit of a coincidence, but thought nothing of it. However, the very next day after leaving Big Nice Studio, my phone rang. I was invited to go on tour across America with a band called The Big Lonesome as their drummer. The synchronicity was starting to feel very weird, but I was way too excited at the chance to go on my first US tour to get caught up in it.

Fast forward to the following spring. I was on my second US tour with The Big Lonesome, standing at the salad bar at a Whole Foods in South Carolina, when my phone rang again. On the other line was my mom's childhood friend, GRAMMY-winning music producer Al Gomes. Al had heard about my recent rise in the local music scene and wanted me to join his artist roster for the upcoming season. Not only that, but he wanted to submit my original music to the GRAMMY Awards. I could feel the hair on my arms beginning to stand up as he spoke. When he told me the name of his company, I nearly dropped my freshly made vegan salad: *Big Noise.*

From that moment on, it was crystal clear to me what I had to do. It came as an incredibly delightful shock that this "go big" prophecy of mine had come true. It was my first taste of manifestation in the literal sense. The universe had shown me the signs, and I was ready to go big!

After returning home from the tour, I got right to work with Al and his team. We chose one of my original songs to record in a professional studio and submit for the 2020 GRAMMY Awards. We settled on the song "Safe as We Can." I had written the song back in college while I was struggling to find my way and get through my business degree program. Five years later, my life was almost unrecognizable. I spent two months in the studio making this song as good as it could possibly be with esteemed sound engineer Alex Krepkikh, while playing all the instruments on the track myself. Luckily, my hard work paid off in a *big* way!

I will never forget that Thursday afternoon phone call from Al that changed my life forever.

"We did it!" he exclaimed.

Al informed me that "Safe as We Can" had actually made the official GRAMMY Awards ballot for best rock song *and* best rock performance! When I hung up the phone, I was so excited I had to run outside and take a lap around my house to burn off some energy. I remember feeling light as a feather while bounding through my yard.

I found out I was competing against the likes of Blink 182, The Smashing Pumpkins, Jack White, Greta Van Fleet, The Black Keys, and of course Paul McCartney! Gary Clark Jr. ended up taking home both GRAMMY Awards I was competing for with his song "This Land," but I am so proud of myself for even being in the competition. The Recording Academy, who processes the GRAMMY submissions and hosts the awards show, asked for a blurb about the song and what it means to me. Here's what I wrote:

"'Safe as We Can' is a rock and roll anthem about the feeling of being so close to your dream and knowing you have to push

through your fear to reach the greatness that lies on the other side. It's a culmination of everything I've been through on my journey as a professional musician. It represents the feelings that drive me and the adventures that continue to fuel my passion for life and music. My hope is that it will inspire others to do something bold with their lives. Bold means different things to different people, but it will always means daring to achieve your dreams. Live your truth and just be yourself!"

I had so much positive momentum going with music, and was ready to host a big release show for my next song, when 2020 happened...

A CREATIVE RESET

As I write this, the entire world is amid lockdowns due to COVID-19. People can't go out to see live music, and musicians and performers of all kinds are really hurting financially. But it's not just the financial aspect. For so many artists, live events and community are what nourish our souls. They help inform our identity and sense of connection.

Since I cannot earn money and express myself in the way I am used to, I decided to use my newfound free time to write this book. I am embracing my role as a storyteller, as someone who conveys vital information to the rest of the tribe through my own experience and creative expression. I wanted to show fellow artists, musicians, and creative people that all hope is not lost, and that our creativity must now flourish in new and exciting ways.

The lessons from the stories you will find in each chapter have helped me overcome every obstacle I've encountered on my path as a musician. It's been an incredibly beneficial exercise in mindfulness to organize all my songs and reflect on the experiences that have shaped my unique perspective as a songwriter. I live my life based on creative expression, but as a musician, I'm not always able to fully express myself. Songs are great, but they often don't tell the whole story.

STORIES AND MYTHS

There are many myths about human existence perpetuated by our modern-day consumerist society, but perhaps the most toxic of all is the myth that life sucks and you're a victim of your environment and everything that happens to you. This myth is essential to the way materialist capitalism functions. Life sucks, and you can't change that, so you need to buy all these things to experience true happiness. Every time we go out or go online, we are bombarded with advertisements attempting to convince us to buy certain products that will undoubtedly help us be happier in life. Many ads are geared toward adding things to your collection of possessions to make your life easier or more stress free.

While some inventions really do enhance our quality of life, most actually complicate our lives even further. But by far, the worst kind of advertisements are the ones that make us feel like we are not good enough as we are. They use psychological marketing tricks to make us believe we need makeup or plastic surgery or new clothes to be acceptable to ourselves and to society. These types of ads try to convince you something is wrong with you, that you are not okay the way you are.

The truth, is people lived happy and healthy lives long before any of these products or services existed. Why? Because happiness is something we cultivate from within, and it starts with gratitude.

Gratitude is the golden key that unlocks our ability to live up to our highest potential.

Gratitude awakens us to the blessings all around us so we can live from a place of abundance, rather than a place of lack. The first step toward achieving a state of gratitude is mindfulness. Mindfulness simply means being aware of what you are doing in the present moment. To be aware of how you are feeling, where you are, and what is happening around you—that is mindfulness.

MINDFUL ARTISTRY

Many people believe famous musicians and rock stars have the perfect life of glory and don't suffer the way "normal" people do. The reality is these artists have often endured so much suffering that the only way they could find peace is through making music. However, a lot of musicians eventually get themselves in a rut because they are not being mindful with their music. They end up writing a song about their pain and depression that becomes a hit because so many people feel that same depression. Then they go on tour and play that song, evoking negative emotions night after night. Now, something that was once healing becomes torture. To me, that's not mindful art.

If you're being a mindful artist, whether you're a musician or creator of any kind, then you're cultivating an awareness of how your art is making you feel. And if your art is making you feel shitty, then frankly it's really not worth doing.

Art is not only about creative expression. It's also about healing, and good music heals the people listening to it. My music is medicine for people who need healing.

But let's be honest—we are all people who need healing. That is the primary reason why I've continued to make music in a mindful way. I realized I have the power to heal myself and those around me through songwriting. While commercial art and music use shiny objects and catchy tunes to placate people and distract them from hearing their own inner voice, mindful art and music amplify that inner voice. And as that inner voice becomes louder and clearer, we wake up to our own ability to express our emotions. Rather than turning on the radio to hear what's already been said, we reach into our hearts and minds and create something new.

OUR CREATIVE POWER

Each person possesses the ability to shape the reality around them with their thoughts and actions. This power is amplified even further by expressing those thoughts and feelings creatively through music or art.

Unfortunately, many people believe they can't play music or they're not artistically inclined. This is an example of what's called a "limiting belief" in psychology. Some people still insist on owning these self-limiting beliefs despite how much they love art and music.

Maybe you tried to learn an instrument as a child and didn't feel like you were succeeding. Maybe you played an instrument with some success, but then had an embarrassing moment that turned you off from trying again. Or, and this one is the worst, maybe you were once really good at singing, playing an instrument, or creating art, until someone stole your thunder by criticizing your dreams or abilities.

If you are one of these people, then this book is for you. It may seem like the safe choice to play it small and let other people do the creating. But, in reality, the only safe choice is to follow your heart.

When you fully embrace your art, you begin to unleash your true potential in life. The way I see it, if art is decorating space, then music is decorating time. By practicing mindfulness in your art or music, you have the potential to make your time on this earth more beautiful—for all of us.

So . . .

Give yourself permission to create!

"Music gives a soul to the universe, wings to the mind, flight to the imagination, and life to everything."

—PLATO

HOW TO READ/LISTEN TO THIS BOOK

———

I have arranged these songs, for the most part, in chronological order of their writing, to show my journey and growth as a songwriter. On the left, as well as on the back cover, you will find a QR code you can scan with your phone's camera. This will take you to my website, where you can listen to the songs. It's up to you as the reader to decide whether you want to listen to the song first or read the chapter first. You could also read the chapter while listening to the song if you so desire or change up the order each time. Do whatever your heart tells you to do! Music, like all art, is a subjective experience. My words may mean something different to you than they do to me, and that's the beauty of creative expression. Enjoy!

WALK OUT THE DOOR

Walk out the door, and wave goodbye
to the chance of livin' a normal life like any other guy
you've got this chore, to satisfy
but you've gotta learn to walk before you can learn how to fly

Don't try and hide behind your little white lies
I can see inside your mind, where your soul resides
it's up to you to choose whether you win or lose
so don't be a fool, don't forget the golden rule

The grass is greener on the other side
but you've gotta hop the fence
you'll never know what life can be like
if you remain content

Don't ever settle for what's been done
if you ever wanna have any fun
it's okay to meddle and break the rules
and sometimes it's okay to steal the jewels

Rise above that "who? what? when?"
and focus on the hour at hand
push and shove and don't give in
and you'll find that strength comes from within!

So walk out the door, and wave goodbye
to the chance of livin' a normal life like any other guy
you've got this chore, to satisfy
but you've gotta learn to walk before you can learn how to fly

Don't be afraid to step on toes
don't be afraid to challenge your foes
Go be the kink in garden hose
and amazingly your garden still grows

Rise above that "who? what? when?"
and focus on the hour at hand
push and shove and don't give in
and you'll find that strength comes from within!

"Go confidently in the direction of your dreams! Live the life you've imagined. As you simplify your life, the laws of the universe will be simpler."

—HENRY DAVID THOREAU

I have always felt, since I was a child, that I was destined for something great. Something "big." However, I was never quite able to put my finger on what that something would be. I had aspired to be a professional athlete, a scientist, a roller coaster designer, and a ninja, among other professions. We are all so imaginative and open-minded as children, but as we grow older, we gain independence by identifying with different beliefs, attitudes, and perspectives.

Success comes to mean something slightly different for each person. When it came time for my eighth-grade class to receive our superlatives, my classmates voted me "most likely to be successful." It was basically the superlative reserved for the nerdiest kid in class, which I most certainly was. I had wanted something cooler, like most athletic, class clown, or most creative. Little did I know, that superlative was a prophecy in the making.

Sun Studios in Memphis, Tennessee was the birthplace of rock and roll. I was on my way to play a show in San Antonio, Texas, traveling with my friend and touring partner, Andreas, when I realized we would be traveling right through Memphis with a few hours to spare. I had heard the stories, but nothing could compare to the experience I was about to have.

It was January 22, 2020. There I was, standing in the exact same spot on the floor where Johnny Cash himself had stood to record his world-famous song "I Walk the Line." To my left was the old piano where Jerry Lee Lewis had frustratedly burned a hole into one of the keys with his cigar. Behind me sat a vintage Ludwig drum set that the band U2 had donated to the studio thirty years prior. In front of me, a picture of Elvis Presley hung on the wall, right behind the spot, marked by an X on the floor, where he stood singing his breakout hit "That's Alright Mama." I couldn't believe where I was standing.

Breaking my haze of astonishment was a kind hand extended out before me:

"Pretty cool, isn't it? My name's Bill, and you?"

"Nate...Nate Jones," I said.

Bill Drenas, a music historian who happened to be the only other musician in our tour group, was from Lowell, Massachusetts. We talked for a few minutes about the surreal and incredible feeling of being in that room, as well as the synchronicity of meeting each other (Lowell is one hour from where I grew up in Rhode Island).

Upon learning that Bill was a bass player, Mr. Graham Winchester, a local Memphis musician and our tour guide that day, handed Bill the upright bass that belonged to the studio. Bill began plucking the strings of the bass to the melody of "Green Onions" by Booker T and the MG's, one of the most iconic pieces of instrumental music to ever come out of Memphis! When Graham recognized the tune, he ran over to the piano that bore the burned insignia of Lewis' cigar, and soon they were groovin' together!

My eyes fixated back on that drum set, but there was one problem—no drumsticks. After realizing there was also no seat, I was unsure of what to do. I asked Graham if it would be alright for me to play the drums lightly with my hands. Without skipping a beat on the piano, he gave me a smile and a nod. I began kicking the bass drum while standing up and keeping a simple groove on the snare with my hands. I remembered having a guitar pick in my pocket, which I dug out and used to evoke some sound out of the cymbals. Before I knew it, we had settled nicely into the groove of the song. My friend Andreas, hardly believing his eyes and his ears, pulled out his phone to record us.

The jam lasted only a few minutes, but it ended with a three-way handshake between Graham, Bill, and myself that solidified the incredible moment. I was so high on adrenaline, it didn't hit me until a few minutes later that I had just joined a very special club of musicians who had played in that room. If I had not had the courage to act and not given myself permission to create, I would have missed out on the chance to join that club. If I had let fear and indecision get the better of me that day, there would be no story. After we wrapped things up in the recording room, we were then introduced to John Schön, the current owner of Sun Studios. After some great conversation, we all posed for a picture together before Andreas and I made our way to Texas.

What followed was one of the most exhilarating car rides of my life. Both Andreas and I could not believe what had just happened. I could barely hang on to the steering wheel because my hands were shaking with genuine excitement. Had I really just jammed in the room where Johnny Cash, Elvis, Carl Perkins, Jerry Lee Lewis, and countless others had recorded their gold records? We were discussing how it would be impossible to convey the epic nature of what we had just experienced to our friends and family.

I was in the middle of recording some songs back home for an upcoming acoustic album and was wrestling with different ideas on how I could creatively release the new material.

Andreas mentioned something about how it would be cool to have a physical book of lyrics to offer as part of the digital release, similar to the way bands used to put their lyrics and photos inside albums and CDs. Him saying that stimulated a thought: What if I compiled a book of stories to go along with my songs?

We agreed immediately that an account of the experience at Sun Studios that day belonged in the book. Just as I was delighted by hearing the stories of Johnny Cash and Elvis, my fans would also be excited to learn more about my experiences as an artist that have led me to where I am today. Was I scared to embark on this book writing journey? You bet I was! Revealing the thoughts and feelings we hold inside can be terrifying. But I knew it was time for me to walk out the door, to take a deep dive into the soul of my inner artist and create without letting fear hold me back.

When we act with courage and creativity in the present moment, we can begin to create our ideal reality based on our artistic expression of truth.

Imagine if I had let fear guide me that day? I might have sat back and watched two fabulous musicians play on these incredible instruments, all the while anticipating, hesitating, and wondering about the drums. Instead, I gave myself permission to create, and the synchronicities haven't stopped!

So...

GIVE YOURSELF PERMISSION TO CREATE!

"You are an explorer, and you represent our species, and the greatest good you can do is to bring back a new idea, because our world is endangered by the absence of good ideas. Our world is in crisis because of the absence of consciousness."

—TERENCE MCKENNA

FLY

—

Back to your fairytale,
that's where I'm sendin' you now
You can't escape the truth,
that's why you're feelin' blue now
People walk around
with shackles on their hearts
Seems they're goin' through their lives
just readin' off the cards

But I will fly
I will touch the sky, and I will die
But first I'll fly
You will see me in the nether-days of our lives

Put down your gossip books
and look up at the stars
The only moment that we have
is where we are
Have no fear for what is lost
and what is found
Everybody's hopes and dreams

come crashin' to the ground

But I will fly
I will touch the sky and, I will die
But first I'll fly
You will see me in the nether-days of our lives

"Don't ask what the world needs. Ask what makes you come alive and go do it. Because what the world needs is people who have come alive."

—HOWARD THURMAN

The door opened. As it did, my entire mental state shifted so rapidly I could barely breathe. My entire body, every ounce of my physiology, told me to stay as far away from that door as possible. I was feeling the physical warning signs of imminent danger. The whipping of the wind was so deafening I could barely hear myself think. Due to the circumstances, I had no choice but to get closer, and closer, and closer, and finally it was time to jump...

If you're reading this, there's a good chance you've been on an airplane before. However, there's a much smaller chance you've been on an airplane with the door open! Luckily, in my case, it was by choice—I had paid to go skydiving with a friend!

It was a cool fall day in Newport, Rhode Island—October 12, 2015, to be exact. I had called my friend Andrea the day before, and on a whim, she agreed to go skydiving with me. We had talked about how it was something we both had always wanted to do. It was going to be the first time for both of us. I recall experiencing a feeling of child-like delight as the plane rose higher and higher in a circular pattern above our drop zone. I could actually see around the curvature of the earth as we flew about ten thousand feet into the sky. As the plane rose, my excitement soared, and with it came a feeling of gratitude for the opportunity to participate in this incredible experience. As soon as the door opened, however, those emotions gave way to a feeling of sheer terror. I thought I was prepared for what was about to happen... I was *very* wrong!

From an early age, I have always loved the feeling of flying. Whether I was riding the Superman roller coaster at Six Flags amusement park, speeding downhill on my bike, or swinging so high I got dizzy, there's just something amazing about feeling the whirl of wind in your hair. I've always been an adrenaline junkie, and in high school I fell in love with pole vaulting, which combines a sprint and a jump to catapult the athlete over a very high bar. Time slows down while you're in the air. As you float back down onto the soft mats after clearing the bar, the universe seems to stand still. To me, it is the feeling of freedom. Any worries or cares I have just melted away in those moments, and I experienced the pure bliss of being alive. Skydiving, however, was nothing I could have been prepared for.

The moment I jumped from the plane, my anxiety took a back seat to the rush of positively charged adrenaline flowing through my veins. Not only was the view incredible, but the sheer intensity of moving at terminal velocity—9.8 meters/second2, to be exact—was more powerful than anything I had ever experienced at that point in my life. The wind was whipping my hair back and forth as I dropped toward the ground with ever increasing speed. It was life affirming, to say the least.

I was strapped into the harness with my instructor, a guy who goes by the name of "Nicky Sideburns." Yes, he had awesome sideburns. When Nicky pulled our parachute, the change of speed was so drastic it felt like an enormous gorilla had yanked me thirty feet backward in a single instant. However, I quickly adjusted to the more casual descent toward planet Earth and felt a sensation of calm ease and relaxation. I can vividly recall how amazing the sunshine felt on my skin as we floated the rest of the way down to the ground. I felt calm and blissful, soaking up every second of altitude. When we landed, I was greeted by Andrea, who had jumped first.

"Wow, dude, that was so epic!" she exclaimed.

"Most epic day of my life!" I yelled back.

We high-fived and hugged and couldn't stop giggling like little kids, most likely because of the rush of endorphins flowing through our bodies.

I remember Andrea laughing at the fact I proceeded to lay in the grass for a solid ten minutes after we landed. Eventually she gave in and joined me, and we started talking about the experience.

"I have never felt more thankful and aware of this beautiful ground I've walked on every day of my life. It suddenly seems so much more important than before," I said to her.

She agreed, adding it was by far the most epic thing she'd ever done!

It's hard sometimes to appreciate the things we take for granted, especially the very things that support us every step of our journey. I walked away from that day with a new perspective, accompanied by a profound sense of gratitude for our beautiful planet. Most notably, however, I gained a deeper awareness of the things that make me come alive.

BORN TO FLY

A month before writing this chapter, I found out the first time I was on an airplane was actually before I was born.

How cool! I thought.

In May 1993, my parents flew to Turks and Caicos in the Caribbean Islands for one last vacation before I burst onto the scene. Perhaps that is why I have always loved flying and being in the air. I know my future involves flying, either as a pilot of some type of recreational aircraft or in an adventure sport of some kind. Since going skydiving, I have gone hang-gliding twice, and I honestly like it even better! Instead of being so overcome with the speed and adrenaline, you actually have time to think and breathe and reflect on the beauty of the moment.

Flying is a wonderful metaphor for higher aspirations in life. Personally, I love the way my consciousness can soar when I am up high looking down on and observing landscapes. For me, it really is the feeling of complete freedom. The only other activity that fills me with this sense of limitless power and joy is playing music—specifically, singing.

When I sing, powerfully and truly, it is the unleashing of the creativity of the universe. I channel through my body the yearning and expression of all voices, all souls, all desires, and all dreams. I sing for the birds and the bees, the elderly, and the eager hopes and dreams of children who do not yet believe in the limitations their predecessors insist are set by the universe. Here's the thing: The universe does not set limitations. *The limit does not exist!*

I am an effortless creator. I am building this particular sector of the universe. I am the architect who gets to design this experience of reality around me. Whenever I come to a fork in the road or a bridge to cross, it is only there because my actions have brought me there. It is only present in my reality because the scenario of the present moment is continuously created through manifesting my truest desires into existence.

But it's not just me. As human beings, we are *all* effortless creators. We each contribute our unique perspective to the whole, thus ushering in the novelty of the future with every passing second.

Whatever **you** *create is the latest, greatest testament to the ingenuity of the human race.*

I once heard a person say you shouldn't ask yourself what the world needs. You should instead ask your soul what makes it come alive because what the world needs most is people who have come alive! Another person told me you can find your purpose in life at the crossroads of what you love and what the world needs. Both sentiments are equally valid and can help orient us to our life's highest purpose.

So, don't be afraid to fly because you are far more powerful than you give yourself credit for. What makes you come alive? Make a list of activities that give you a feeling of limitless freedom, connection, and empowerment. Do more of those things! It doesn't matter if you or others consider yourself good at something. What matters is that you are enjoying yourself and having fun. You are spending time being your most authentic self, which will help you become clearer in your mission and purpose so you can lead the life you've always wanted. Give yourself permission to soar!

"Once you have tasted flight, you will forever walk the earth with your eyes turned skyward, for there you have been, and there you will always long to return."

—LEONARDO DA VINCI

DEATH IS AT THE DOOR

———

These hardships I face, with a smile,
and the grace of my heart
knowing that nothing in this world
can tear me apart
for I am one with the snow and the rain,
and only the wind, can heal my pain

The light shows the way
but it darkens the day once we know
that all that we see will be crushed,
like debris in the road
but let not your fear take the wheel
and steer you astray, for one more day

Because death is at the door,
and it feels like nothing more,
than a lullaby singing me to sleep

I won't feel so afraid,
Knowing sunshine causes shade,
And the rivers run

with tears that we weep

I said death is at the door,
And it feels like nothing more,
Than a lullaby singing me to sleep

I won't feel so afraid,
Knowing sunshine causes shade,
And the rivers run
with tears that we weep...

"Try to imagine what it will be like to go to sleep and never wake up... Now try to imagine what it was like to wake up having never gone to sleep!"

—ALAN WATTS

It all happened so fast. All I wanted was to get to work on time, but I nearly lost everything. It was a bleak February afternoon, and the roads were covered with a thin layer of snow that masked scattered sheets of black ice. It was also my first winter with my driver's license, and I was speeding. As I drove past the parking lot of my old church and school, I took the turn as I had on any other day. However, as soon as I hit the curve, the rear tires on my car fishtailed into the curb, causing the front end to veer into the left lane. I was headed straight for oncoming traffic.

In a moment of sheer terror, I made a desperate attempt to avoid collision and swerved back to the right. I let out a huge sigh and began to regain composure when suddenly I heard a *thump!* I had hit the snowbank on the side of the road, and before I knew it, my car was airborne. For a few seconds, the vehicle was not touching the ground at all. There was a prolonged moment of complete silence as I soared through the air and plowed onto the front lawn of the church. Everything seemed to be going by me in slow motion. I felt an ominous tingling sensation shoot down my spine as I closed my eyes and braced for impact.

When I opened my eyes, I was in shock. The events that had just occurred seemed surreal. I was questioning the reality of my circumstances and could not believe I wasn't dreaming. "This isn't happening, this isn't happening," I repeated to myself. Immediately, I began checking my arms and legs to make sure I wasn't hurt or bleeding. Luckily, the snowfall had totaled eighteen inches, so my landing was cushioned. As I began to regain consciousness of my surroundings, I noticed the car had landed within mere feet of a memorial garden I had helped build. The memorial was in remembrance of a girl from my church who had died in a car accident on that very same road just three years earlier. The thought of what could have happened rendered me speechless and reflective as I literally thanked God for sparing my life.

I was grateful to even be alive, let alone unscathed. People who had seen the accident were getting out of their cars and asking me if I was alright. "Yes," I said, "I'm totally fine." It really did seem like a miracle from God—or whoever was watching over me that day. I got back in my car and attempted to back out onto the road, but to no avail. My tires weren't even touching the ground.

At that moment panic set in as I realized I needed a tow. I knew I would not make it to work, and I would need to contact my parents and the AAA insurance company. I became sick to my stomach at the thought of my parents' reaction to what had happened. Fortunately, they were not as mad I had anticipated. Their concern for my safety greatly outweighed the need to scold me for my foolishness.

After all was said and done, I owed the tow company eighty-two dollars, got a verbal shellacking, and was two-and-a-half hours late to work. I did, however, learn a few valuable lessons.

The first was that life is precious and delicate. Everything can be gone in an instant if you're not careful. I learned that rather than speeding to work, all I needed to do was leave the house a few minutes earlier. In addition, even though I had stopped going to church, I felt some force that I'd like to think was God had intervened that day and saved me from certain injury, if not death. There was an eerie connection between my accident and the events that led to the creation of the memorial garden. It seemed as though I had a guardian angel watching over me and keeping me safe. Whatever it was, it moved me. I felt I had been spared that day because I was destined to do something very important with my life that I had still not yet achieved.

TRANSCENDING DEATH

At a recent plant medicine retreat I attended, I met a fascinating guy named Steve. He is a student of the Modern Mystery School, which instills spiritual wisdom through the study of the ancient alchemical arts. Dusk was settling in, and we were all sitting around the fire when Steve shared an incredibly profound ancient Cherokee proverb with everyone. It went as follows:

"When you were born, you cried,
and the world rejoiced.
Live your life so that when you die,
the world cries and you rejoice."

We all repeated it a few times together, and I felt my emotions changing with every word we chanted. I suddenly understood that while the deaths of others around me brought feelings of grief and sadness, the inevitability of my own death need not stir the same feelings within me. A weight seemed to be lifted off my shoulders. I felt a certain sense of calm unlike any I had ever known. Poetry, like this ancient song, can transport the listener to realms of understanding far beyond that of everyday consciousness. Many days, weeks, and months later, I am still floored by the sagacious sentiment these words illustrate.

Death is just as normal and just as natural as birth—so why we do we fear it? One argument is we are compelled by our biological instincts to fear our own death, that we are naturally "hard wired" to want to conserve energy and avoid pain so our species will have the best chance of survival. Another argument is that our emotional faculties compel us to fear death. We can't help but feel sad when a friend or loved one passes away because it represents the end of a relationship. This fear of death creeps into our societal structures and makes us try to hold on to everything and create ultimate security.

In school we are taught we must finish our education, get a degree, work, attain financial security, start a family, and work for many more years, and then we finally get to retire— but only once we've saved enough money to be ensure our security. This is a bleak misrepresentation of what life as a human being is truly about. The comforting truth—a truth most schools don't teach—is that nothing is secure because everything in nature is constantly changing and transforming into new things. We know energy cannot be destroyed; it can only change forms. As you read this, the paper this page is made of is slowly decaying, slowly changing forms. Some of these processes take hundreds, thousands, or millions of years—and some take only seconds. What makes these changes seem undesirable in certain cases is our limited perspective. When we die, the energy being used to power our body now manifests itself as a different form of energy, but all this energy is still within the collective field of vibration.

Many people believe we are simply here on Earth by accident, by chance. But the truth I have come to know with absolute certainty through altered states of consciousness is that we are here to learn. We live in an intelligent universe, and we are not separate from that intelligence. Being born as Nate Jones to my particular set of parents allowed me to cultivate the opportunity to create harmony in the world through music. Life as Nate Jones presented the perfect level of challenge to help my soul achieve higher levels of cosmic enlightenment.

I understand now why my soul chose to experience this human life, to go through the trials and tribulations that come with humanity, and in the process learn and grow. Mortality is an illusion. The body is a temporary vessel for the mind, allowing universal intelligence to experience itself through the lens of the individual perspective.

"This place is but a dream. Only a sleeper considers it real. Then, death comes like dawn, and you wake up laughing at what you thought was your grief."

—RUMI

ALWAYS WAITIN'

You and I, we've seen the way
That our bodies crumble
We might fall down from the pain
If we can't stay humble

Comin' to you in a dream
All the needs of the many
Things just aren't what they seem
So you feel unready

Take a step into the fray,
All the lights are fadin'
We will never find the way,
If we're always waitin'

Waitin', waitin'
waitin', waitin'

I don't mind a little pain
If it keeps me goin'
You and I we've seen the way,

But we'd never know it

"The mind is the hidden organ of the human body. When you take psychedelics, you see this hidden organ, you exercise it, you move into it. And it's a very strange organ because it has this higher dimensional quality to it. But it's part of human-ness, it can't be taken away from it."

—TERENCE MCKENNA

On February 23, 2017, I had an out-of-body experience that changed my life forever. It was so profoundly transformative and earth shattering that I divide my life into two halves. There was everything that happened before that day, and everything after. I existed in a dimension of experience science cannot yet explain. Tibetan monks refer to the place I experienced as the "bardo." The monks say this place is the furthest we can go as humans without crossing over to the other side. They maintain that this place is accessible through many hours of deep meditation, a practice that has been known to cause the brain to release a unique compound called DMT.

For those of you who don't know, DMT is short for N-Dimethyltryptamine. It is a chemical neurotransmitter found in almost all plant species and many mammals, including humans. It is also the active ingredient in Ayahuasca, the Amazonian soul-healing brew. About one year prior to this experience, I came across an intriguing documentary on Netflix called *DMT: The Spirit Molecule*. The film was made in conjunction with a book by Dr. Rick Strassman titled *DMT:*

The Spirit Molecule—A Doctor's Revolutionary Research into the Biology of Near-Death and Mystical Experiences.

Simply put, this film blew me away. It chronicles a series of research experiments conducted by Dr. Strassman at Stanford University in which participants were voluntarily injected with DMT. Invariably, the subjects found themselves leaving the earthly realm behind and traveling to a mysterious place outside of three-dimensional space and time. Every single participant in the study reported making contact with some form of higher intelligence, while some even reported interacting with other conscious beings. Many claimed they had encountered what could only be described as God.

There was one consistent, overarching theme to every account: love.

But let's get back to *my* experience. I had gotten a job working for a remote online startup at the time I watched Dr. Strassman's film. Several weeks later, I was having a casual conversation with a Cape Verdean man named Jayf who worked in the same building. Our conversation happened to drift toward the wonders of the universe, as conversations with me frequently do. I mentioned learning about DMT and how incredible it seemed.

To my surprise, Jayf was very familiar with what I was talking about. In fact, he'd experienced it himself. He even told me he could help me find some. I was ecstatic. He gave me his number and told me to text him when I was ready. When I told Sam, my bandmate and best friend of seventeen years, this was going down, he said he would love to join. Apparently, he also knew Jayf…

I contacted Jayf several times over the next few months, and each time he told me, "Soon." I was beginning to grow impatient, but I was dedicated to having this experience. I wanted to feel for myself what countless others had described as the most incredible moment of their life, and I wasn't ready to give up. Due to my persistence, Jayf finally arranged a time for us to meet. He told me to show up calm, relaxed, and with an open mind. That was no problem for me, until Sam texted me that same day saying he got called into work and couldn't make it. Admittedly, I felt a lot more anxious going alone, but I found the courage to proceed.

When I arrived, Jayf apologized for holding out on me for so long. "I wanted to make sure you really were a seeker, not just looking to get high." When he said this, I instantly felt my confidence return. *I am a seeker,* I told myself. I had a genuine interest in what DMT could teach me. Nothing ventured, nothing gained!

While he was finishing preparing the DMT, Jayf told me to do some yoga and find my center. Within minutes I was totally relaxed and ready to go. He pulled up a music video on his computer and instructed me to watch and pay attention. The song was called "Great Spirit," and it was written by an artist I had never heard of named Nahko Bear. I found the song quite beautiful, although the video was a bit cryptic and mysterious. He told me to let it sink in and we would begin in a moment. Since it was still light outside, we went into the hallway of his home and closed the doors to the other rooms. There was just enough light to see each other's faces at close range. He instructed me to take three *big* hits off the pipe if I wanted the full experience.

"Champions will get it in two," he joked.

I remember both that comment and my response so vividly.

"I've smoked a lot of weed, Jayf. I got this."

"It's going to be harder than you think," he said. "After the first one, you're gonna feel like you can't do it again, but you have to do it to break through. Otherwise, you're just gonna feel really, really stoned."

"Okay," I said.

Nothing could have prepared me for what happened next.

When I breathed in the first hit, I instantly felt a sensation I had never experienced before. The entire fabric of reality seemed to expand as I inhaled. Even more peculiarly, the exact opposite happened as I exhaled; everything contracted back down. Not only was I picking up new information in my visual field, but I could also feel the expansion and contraction in my body. On my inhale, I felt light as a feather, and on the exhale, I felt the force of one hundred Gs... The sound of my breath was also noticeably louder.

It was like my lungs were an accordion, and my breath was controlling the density of the fabric of reality.

I barely had the strength to take a second hit, but when I did, it triggered the single strangest moment of my life. Once again, my inhale caused everything around me to expand, but as I exhaled, everything disappeared. It was as if the curtain on the stage of life had dropped, and the show was gone. I recall becoming aware of myself as pure vibration. I was fully conscious in this formless place.

I was existing as part of some sort of grid like pattern of light and dark, with no colors or depth of field. This eventually led me into what felt like an expansive landscape with a dome over it. My eyes were not open, but I was seeing many things in my mind. It was similar to a dream in the sense I didn't remember how I had gotten there. No part of me remembered I had just smoked DMT, just like you don't remember you just went to sleep while you are dreaming. I just knew I was there, and I knew it was a place I had never experienced before. Something about it felt very serene and oddly familiar, as if I had been there before. It felt like I was being clued into something I was not aware of before, but somehow made perfect sense.

I saw the all-seeing eye atop a pyramid, exactly like the iconic Freemason symbol from the back of the US dollar bill. I also saw the path of my future in rock and roll ascending upward, leading my soul to its highest expression. In that moment, I felt a deep sense of trust that I was on the right path. Far on my left in my periphery, I perceived the face of my spiritual mentor, philosopher Alan Watts. He was teasing me with a sly, playful look, as if to say, "Don't kid yourself, we've always known each other. It's good to see you again." The more I saw, the more I realized this was a place of incredible love. Something about it felt heavenly, like I was home.

For the first time in my life, I felt like I was with God.

I felt the presence and energy of God in a way so real, I didn't think it was possible—and I felt it inside myself. Some call it God, some call it spirit or source. It was the most powerful thing I've ever encountered. The fact that I could access it from within myself was truly a paradigm shift for me. Legendary philosopher and scientist Terence McKenna once described his first DMT experience as the news he was always waiting for. I had never identified with a single statement more in my entire life.

BEHIND THE VEIL

As I settled into this feeling of comfort and bliss, I began noticing more and more things happening. Answers to questions I didn't even know I had began appearing before the question had even been fully formed in my mind. This eventually became a bit overwhelming, however, and the thoughts gave way to an unsettled feeling. I remember going through all the problems and current worries I had in my life. I thought about how I was struggling to find enough gigs as a musician to pay my bills. I realized how much hard work and suffering life involves. On top of that, my uncle Al had just been placed in a nursing home with dementia, and I found myself grieving for him.

This led to a direct confrontation with my own mortality. At that moment, an interesting thing happened. The realization that I was going to die suddenly gave me immense joy. There was a way out! A way out from all the pain, suffering, loss, and grief. I became aware I had nothing to fear. This awareness reassured me I was in the very place I would go to when I died, and it was a place of pure love.

It felt like I was peeking behind the veil that cloaks reality. We know energy disguises itself in various forms, many of which appear solid and lifeless to us. But in this place, the energy was vibrant, fully present, and unmistakably conscious. At this moment, I started to become aware of my body in the physical plane. My mind was still in this other realm, but my stomach felt like it was going to throw up.

At that moment, I heard a comforting voice over my shoulder. It was the voice of my best friend Sam. "It's okay man. It's good to throw up; it's like a purge. You're purging that negative energy out!" It was clear as day. *Wow,* I thought, *Sam must have shown up!* However, to my absolute astonishment, when I came back to regular consciousness and opened my eyes, Sam was not there. At least, not physically. All I could see was Jayf.

"Oh, you're back!" he said.

His eyes were piercing through the shadowy darkness of the hallway. I then realized I could see the veins in his forehead glowing iridescent blue underneath his dark skin. Seeing this absolutely blew my mind. As I looked around more, I realized reality had a very different appearance than usual. As I stood up and walked toward the light, I saw bright colors tracing the borders of the physical objects in my visual field. I could see numbers and unfamiliar geometric symbols adorning the archways and angles of the house's structure. It was almost like wearing 3D glasses, but much more vibrant and saturated with information. Although I could not interpret what I was seeing, I could tell it had meaning and made perfect sense. It felt like I was seeing the blueprints of reality, things normally hidden to the human eye.

That's when the memory of my experience came rushing back like remembering a dream. The ineffable nature of my journey was now present in my mind's eye. I had never been so cognizant and so perplexed at the same time. *How was this possible?* I thought to myself.

EXPERIENCING THE ANSWERS TO ALL OF LIFE'S QUESTIONS IN SEVEN MINUTES

At this moment, the lyrics of the song "The Seeker" by The Who popped into my head. I was a seeker, I had been searching low and high, and now I finally understood from real-life experience I would not find what I was after until the day I died.

It felt as if I'd learned and seen and felt enough truth to fill a thousand lifetimes, but when I looked at the clock, only seven minutes of real time had passed. Seven minutes? It seemed totally impossible! How could an experience so powerful yet so brief even exist at all?

I walked over to the sink to splash some water on my face and wash my hands, still integrating back into the world around me. Through the window, I noticed a man walking outside. He was clearly getting home from work, walking inside from his car while holding a briefcase. Without warning, a feeling of pure, unconditional love washed over me. Here was someone just living their life, but I could feel his soul as strongly as I had just felt mine. I felt so much love for this stranger I began to weep tears of pure happiness. It was one of the most beautiful moments of my life.

My tears then turned to ecstatic laughter. I felt the strength I needed to press onward in my life. I felt determined to keep playing music and make it work full time. I had seen the path of my rock and roll destiny laid out before me. I knew what I had to do. I had to trust myself, pursue my music, and explore my creativity. I had to express my love for those around me in new and deeper ways. Most importantly, I had to keep developing my skills with music so I could share this gift with others.

AWAKENING FROM WITHIN: THE DMT GATEWAY

After this awakening from within, I began researching DMT and learned some truly incredible things.

- First, DMT is produced in the brain while we dream.

- Second, the moment an infant passes through the birth canal, it triggers an endogenous release of DMT in both mother and child. Coincidence? I think not!

- Thirdly, an endogenous release of DMT is the main reason people have out-of-body experiences when they are resuscitated from the brink of death!

As it turns out, the pineal gland, commonly referred to as the "third eye," is responsible for these secretions of DMT into the bloodstream. It was all starting to make sense. This chemical is not special in and of itself; it's just a molecular compound. However, when activated in the human body, it allows us a deeper look into who and what we really are.

In the wake of this experience, I had started to call it life altering. But in that moment, I realized something: Life had not actually been altered in any way. This experience was always possible physiologically. It was simply my perspective that had been altered. As a very intellectually confident and curious person, I was pretty sure I understood myself. But DMT showed me, unequivocally, that there are far more layers of ourselves than we normally perceive.

The only thing I could do with my newfound insight was to write a song. I gave myself permission to embrace my feelings and create something with them, rather than subdue the feeling of truth that now burned brightly within me. This song helped me to make sense of the cosmic wisdom and insight I had received on my journey. It is an expression of how deeply moved I was by this experience. In an attempt to find more insight from others who had also seen what I saw, I searched online for relevant stories or quotes. This statement from renown psychopharmacology expert and chemist Alexander Shulgin perfectly sums up what I was feeling at the time.

"The most compelling insight of that day was that this awesome recall had been brought about by a fraction of a gram of a white solid, but that in no way whatsoever could it be argued that these memories had been contained within the white solid. Everything I had recognized came from the depths of my memory and my psyche. I understood that our entire universe is contained in the mind and the spirit. We may choose not to find access to it, we may even deny its existence, but it is indeed there inside us, and there are chemicals that can catalyze its availability."

—ALEXANDER SHULGIN

DMT is a biological gateway to the higher dimensions of our mind, and this gateway exists within each and every one of us. Creative expression is likewise very similar. Not only does it allow us to become more deeply in touch with the truth within us, but it is a power we all possess. Creative expression is a form of meditation on a single feeling or set of feelings within us that expand when put into focus. In this way, we can gain a deeper understanding of our feelings and transform this energy into incredible art and music! When my DMT journey ended, everything suddenly clicked. I knew I was on the right path, and I no longer felt the need to keep seeking answers. It was time to get to work and give myself even more permission to create!

"*Psychedelic experience is only a glimpse of genuine mystical insight, but a glimpse which can be matured and deepened by the various ways of meditation in which drugs are no longer necessary or useful. If you get the message, hang up the phone. For psychedelic drugs are simply instruments, like microscopes, telescopes, and telephones. The biologist does not sit with eye permanently glued to the microscope, he goes away and works on what he has seen...*"

—ALAN WATTS

BACK TO BLUE CLIFF

———

Take a word from the wise my friend,
and tell me what you hear
You gotta let go of all your lies,
and step away from fear
You're finally startin' to recognize,
you gotta let it go
So sit back, relax, unwind,
Don't block the flow

We're goin' back to Blue Cliff, baby,
Just tell me what you see
We're going back to Blue Cliff, baby,
It's got me feelin' free...

Tick, tock on the clock, you stop,
and take a deep breath in,
Let it out, and shed your doubt
Notice the place you're in
Take a good hard look at yourself,
You know you need to heal,
Put all your worries on the shelf,

You got time to steal

We're goin' back to Blue Cliff, baby,
Just tell me what you see
We're going back to Blue Cliff, baby,
it's got me feelin' free
Yea-a!

We're goin' back to Blue Cliff, baby,
Come meditate with me
We're going back to Blue Cliff, baby,
it's got me feelin' free!

"There is no way to happiness—happiness is the way."
—THICH NHAT HANH

Standing in my driveway, with tears streaming down my face, I felt an inner knowing of a higher purpose in life I was not yet in touch with. The girl I thought I was going to spend the rest of my life with had abruptly ended our relationship the night before. I recall saying to my mom, "I need to go do Ayahuasca in the jungle and go to a Buddhist monastery." In my mind were images of Christian Bale in the movie *Batman Begins* training to overcome his past and become a stoic warrior. I knew I needed discipline, and I knew I wanted to escape the culture I had grown up in, at least for a little while. I had this nagging sensation that an incredible adventure awaited me out there in the world, and I wanted to take action toward making it happen.

After calming down and collecting myself, I promptly went inside and opened Google on the computer. I typed "Buddhist monasteries in America" into the search bar and hit enter. To my surprise, I found a list of over ten Buddhist monasteries and temples in the USA. Even better, there was one located a mere three and a half hours away from my house. To my even greater surprise and delight, they had a retreat coming up in just ten days! The only problem was, I had a show scheduled that weekend.

Damn, I thought to myself, *it just wasn't meant to be.* At the time, I really needed those 125 dollars. Not two days later, I received a text from my booking agent Al Salzillo. He let me know due to the Labor Day holiday, the venue had decided to cancel my show. At first, I was upset, but in that moment of annoyance, I remembered the retreat. Sure enough, when I went back online to check, there were still a few spots left! Within half an hour I had booked the ticket, not knowing at the time how that one decision would alter the course of my life forever.

I will never forget the moment I consider to be my first real taste of enlightened consciousness. I was sitting on a cushion on the floor of the big meditation hall, marveling at the amazing architecture of the cathedral style wooden ceiling. It reminded me of what Noah's Ark would have looked like. One of the monks was gently playing acoustic guitar while another led a spoken guided meditation. His French accent soothed me as I allowed my eyes to close and let myself relax into the moment. Despite the incredibly uplifting energy and atmosphere at the monastery, I was still upset over my breakup. But the next words I heard brought me immense comfort and a deep, overwhelming sense of joy.

"In life, we must learn to go as a river," the young monk said.

I became intrigued to find out where this thought might lead. He continued, saying:

"When we allow something to become stuck in our mind, we are like one who enters a river and tries to keep the water from flowing downstream. When we refuse to let go and move on, we cannot receive the new beauty constantly flowing into our lives. There are many wonderful things waiting for us, but we cannot receive them unless we learn to go as a river, not holding on to the hurts of the past. This is why we meditate, to clear our mind and open ourselves to the flow of the present moment."

Wow, I thought to myself, *it really is that simple.*

Immediately, I felt the seed of discontent within my heart dislodge itself. An enormous grin swept across my face, and my body felt light as a feather. It felt as if I had cut the cord with my troubles, allowing them to flow away from me down the river until I could hardly remember their presence. This feeling stayed with me throughout the rest of the weekend, and I found myself being able to call upon it at any moment with a simple deep breath and a smile. Whenever I did that, I would feel the endorphins flowing through my body, creating a sense of peace and relaxation.

A few weeks after my first trip to Blue Cliff, I was invited back to participate in a creative arts retreat for writers, musicians, artists, and creators of all kinds. This retreat was four days instead of three, offering the artists more time to settle into the profound feeling of peace encompassing the atmosphere of the monastery. It was an opportunity to stretch my legs a bit more and embrace the experience on a deeper level. On day three of the retreat, a group of musicians and writers gathered for a workshop in the big meditation hall. One of our first creative assignments was to write a love letter to our current self. I had never done anything like this before and was surprised at how much love I had for myself. Here's what I wrote:

"Dear Nate, you have grown so much and become bigger in mind and spirit than I could ever have imagined. You overcame the ridicule and torment of your childhood. There was never a spot for you at the table and so you built your own. You have tirelessly worked for understanding and love, and you have deepened the experience of life for so many people around you. More and more people offer you compliments and gratitude for your sharing and listening. I'm so proud of you, you've expanded your vocabulary, taught yourself to play many different instruments, and shaped the life you were wanting to live. Don't stop now, or ever! Keep the pen to the paper and write your story. You are hilarious! You make me laugh all the time and you understand that without suffering there would be no humor. I know you can accomplish anything. I believe in you. Don't sell yourself short, value your contributions to the world, they are needed just as much as anyone else's. I love you!"

Looking back on this letter, I am genuinely surprised by how positive it turned out. I had been struggling with feelings of remorse over things I could have done better in my relationship. This letter helped me realize I needed to give that love to myself instead of searching for fulfillment in others. Until I did that, I knew I would not be truly happy.

The following night, the entire group of over one hundred retreat goers, as well as all the monks and nuns, gathered in the big meditation hall to share what we had created and worked on over the weekend. I shared my song "Fly" and received an overwhelmingly positive reaction. Multiple people came up to me after the show to compliment the song and its message, as well as my singing.

I remember being on such a natural high from the weekend, and my emotional state was completely unrecognizable compared to how I had felt just three weeks prior. The love letter to myself, as well as the positive feedback on my performance, proved to me I did indeed possess the confidence and self-love necessary to embrace my musical talent and create without judgment. This creativity eventually helped me write many of the other songs in this book that came after this moment. I was able to use the music to turn over a new leaf in my life.

REBIRTH

Blue Cliff is the place where I was reborn. The transformation I underwent as a result of repeatedly immersing myself in the joyful tradition of mindfulness is nothing short of miraculous. The lessons I learned there helped me discover my life's purpose, which is to change the world with music.

Overcoming my fears, worries, insecurities, and limiting beliefs freed me to live a more authentic life. I no longer felt like a victim, or that other people were out to get me. I was no longer upset with the people who had done me wrong in the past. I was able to tame and reframe my anger and become a much more peaceful person. The cultivation of gratitude for all the blessings in my life allowed me to understand my desires and follow my heart more truly.

I became deeply in touch with the person I really was, underneath all the layers of suffering, trauma, societal conditioning, attitudes, and expectations. When I finally met this person, this person I had always been, it woke me up. It woke me up so much that I truly felt reborn, in the sense that I saw the world through new eyes.

My rebirth came at exactly the right time. I had just started playing music professionally and was gaining more confidence than ever before. The low sense of self-esteem that had hung over my head like a dark cloud since elementary school was finally lifting. I was becoming a man and stepping into my power as a force for positive change in this world.

My time at Blue Cliff gave me the insight necessary to follow my heart and avoid certain toxic aspects of our culture, specifically in my career. The music industry can be a daunting place, but I was now determined to create genuine joy and fun for others while pushing myself outside of my comfort zone. Most importantly, I learned how to accept myself for who I am and how to go with the flow of life so I can more easily create positive change. Rather than dwelling on the situations out of my control, I learned how to come back to the present moment and to notice the many conditions for happiness already present in my life.

Exercises for this Chapter:

1. Sit down in a comfortable place with your shoulders relaxed. Think of something that makes you smile—a person, a place, an animal, a song, a movie, a sunset, anything you deeply enjoy and are grateful for having in your life. Many people think they can't meditate because their mind always wanders. If that's you, try a gratitude meditation like this. If your mind wanders, that's okay. Just keep bringing it back to something you are grateful for.

2. Write a love letter to yourself. Don't hold back. Speak to yourself with the kindness you would show those most important to you. When you are done, read it back to yourself while smiling. Take it out any time you need a reminder of your greatness.

3. Take a walk or drive to a nearby river or other body of water. Rivers offer an excellent opportunity to connect with nature by embracing the flow of all things. Water finds a way to get around obstacles by being flexible rather than rigid. When we learn to flow like the river, our lives become filled with a sense of freedom and ease.

"First you have to focus on the practice of being. Being fresh. Being peaceful. Being attentive. Being generous. Being

compassionate. This is the basic practice. It's as if the other person is sitting at the foot of a tree. The tree does not do anything, but the tree is fresh and alive. When you are like that tree, sending out waves of freshness, you help to calm down the suffering of the other person."

—THICH NHAT HANH

ORGANIC SONG

My life has always been, an organic song
My life has always been, an organic song,
And I sing along, alo-o-o-o-ong, I sing along, alo-o-o-o-ong

People in your past, may've done you wrong
Livin' life too fast, tryin' to be strong
Try and make it last, you're right where you belong!

Just sing along, alo-o-o-o-ong, just sing along, alo-o-o-o-ong

It doesn't matter how, you will find a way
The universe is ours, and it's here to stay
We've all got the power, and we're here to play!

Just sing along, alo-o-o-o-ong, just sing along, alo-o-o-o-ong
Just sing along, alo-o-o-o-ong, just sing along, alo-o-o-o-ong

I just gotta' step back from my self, and catch my breath
People all around this planet, we must not forget
That we live in a society of changes
We're all livin' for that wild feeling of agelessness...

My life has always been, an organic song
My life has always been, an organic song,
And I sing along, alo-o-o-o-ong, I sing along, alo-o-o-o-ong

My life has always been...an organic song

"You are today where your thoughts have brought you; you will be tomorrow where your thoughts take you."

—JAMES ALLEN

"Shhhh," I said quietly, turning to my friend Richard as we rounded the corner of a cobblestone street in Strasbourg, France. "I'm hearing some music," I said. It was still far off in the distance, and I couldn't quite distinguish the sounds I was hearing.

"There are like twenty dance clubs around here Nate," Richard said. "That's probably what you're hearing!"

But as we got closer, I knew exactly what I was hearing. My years of playing drums had trained my ears well enough to recognize that distinct sound from several blocks away. It was a snare drum, the one that rests right between the drummer's legs and makes a *thwack!* noise. I could also tell it was being played live, not on a recorded track.

It was September of 2017, and I had flown to Europe to spend a week with my friend Richard from Germany. At twenty-four years old, this was my first time flying out of the country alone. I got to experience some incredible places and learned so much by stepping outside the box of the only culture I had ever known. We had just summited a huge mountain in the Bavarian Alps of southern Germany on the border of Austria and were on our way to Amsterdam with Richard's friend Rene. We needed a place to stop for the night, and Richard suggested the beautiful, old city of Strasbourg at the eastern edge of France. After searching for live music all night with no luck, I had a hunch we had finally found just what we were looking for.

Sure enough, we found the source of the music after walking a few more blocks. I can still remember the smell of tobacco smoke rising up from below our feet. The small window on the outside of the venue gave a glimpse into the eclectic scene below: people dining, conversing, holding their wine glasses and cigarettes in that oh-so-French way. Almost every head was adorned by a pair of glasses, a beret, or some other artsy piece of flair. It was textbook France, the way I had always imagined it. As we entered, the band was playing their way through several jazz standards, and we realized it was standing room only.

Being the outgoing fellow that I am, I took the time to thank the band when they had finished the song. I made it a point to compliment the drummer on his playing. I told him I was the drummer in my band and that I enjoyed his performance, and the band was very talented. It was at that moment my evening took a most fortuitous and unforeseen turn. Claude, the drummer, thanked me for my compliments, but informed me in broken English they were not a band—it was merely a weekly jam session.

My vibe changed instantly as I realized what he was about to say. Raising the drumsticks before my eager eyes, he asked, "Want to play? I've been dying for a break all evening!" I couldn't believe my luck. He was actually relieved when I answered with a gracious "*Yes*, thank you!" I took the sticks in hand and got behind the drum set. Having been traveling, I hadn't gotten to play drums in over a week!

What followed was one of the sweatiest performances of my life, in more ways than one! I asked the rest of the band if they knew the song "Take Five," a fantastic jazz standard written by world-famous pianist Dave Brubeck in 1959. They all nodded, and as I began playing the opening drum beat of the song, I smiled excitedly at Richard, who was in disbelief as he pulled out his phone to videotape the jam session. In my mind I was a bit nervous, simply because "Take Five" is a song in 5/4 time signature. This means that instead of counting in groups of four, like you would with most popular music, you count to five before the measure resets. You can get a feel for what this is like by clapping it out, or by listening to the song and tapping along! It was still fairly tricky to play at my skill level four years ago, but now it's practically second nature. Nevertheless, I relaxed into the excitement of the moment and nailed it.

When the song finished, the audience in the speakeasy erupted with applause, and I felt like I was walking on air. Moments like this one are what renew my faith that I am always in the right place at the right time. I have countless stories of things like this happening in my life, as I'm sure you do, too. We must let these moments affirm our resolve to follow our dreams and reinforce our belief that we are on the perfectly right path to becoming who we are.

The quote by James Allen at the beginning of this chapter perfectly illustrates how our thoughts lead us forward in life. Allen wrote the seminal book *As a Man Thinketh* in 1903, long before self-help was a recognized literary genre. He believed in the power of thought to shape our reality and encouraged his audience to master the domain of their own minds.

Having the courage to chase one's dream is not easy, but it is much easier than dealing with the regret of missed opportunities. The trick is to train your mind to see each obstacle as a chance for growth, rather than an unfortunate circumstance holding you back. If you can manage to look honestly at yourself and trust in your gifts, you will start to see opportunities where once there were only roadblocks.

When you live your life as the organic song that it is, you are essentially letting the truth play itself.

I started writing this song at 2 a.m. on Halloween night in 2017. I had just gotten home from a costume party at a place called the Mews Tavern. I decided to go on a whim, and I ended up having an amazing time, met someone really cool, and bumped into some old friends. I was working on my finger-picking skills on the guitar, playing a simple chord progression that was soothing to my soul, when the words began to flow out from me. I didn't know where they were coming from, but I just let it happen.

It had been about one month since I'd left Germany, and knowing it would be morning there, I sent a recording of the beginning of the song to Richard. He responded right away saying he loved it and gave me a lot of positive and encouraging feedback. Much to my dismay, however, I couldn't seem to write anything past the first few lines of the song. I decided, in keeping with the title, that I wouldn't force it, and I would let it come to me organically when the time was right.

Several weeks later, my friend and award-winning musician Joanne Lurgio invited me to participate in a songwriter's round. I graciously accepted her invitation. The way it works is several songwriters sit in a half-circle on stage and take turns playing songs to the audience one at a time. They are usually very fun and intimate events where the audience gets to interact with the musicians a lot more than at a regular concert. She was hosting the event at a well-known community music and art space in Providence called AS220. I really wanted to play "Organic Song" but was slightly stressing over not having the lyrics finished. But as fate would have it, I ended up getting a flash of inspiration the night before the show, and the rest of the lyrics flowed out of me in the same organic fashion.

Remember not to strive too hard and work yourself to the bone to accomplish things in life. The right experiences will unfold in your life naturally and organically as you continue to orient yourself toward what truly matters to you in your heart.

Trust your intuition. Let it guide you toward your dreams, and then surrender to the flow. If you follow these three steps, nothing in life that is truly meant for you, whether it be a person, an opportunity, a job, or anything else, will pass you by. And if it does, there is no need for worry, because each experience is a part of the organic song of your life!

"The visions you glorify in your mind, the ideals you enthrone in your heart...this you will build your life by...this you will become."

—JAMES ALLEN

SAIL AWAY

When you sail away
you're gonna say
It's better off that way

If you find the time
to change your mind
Then you can live another day

But I've got to rearrange
I like to keep it strange
I like to feel the change...
When it rains...

Knew it wouldn't be long
til' she was gone
And I was on my own

Life ain't how it seems
and when you dream
You step away from what you've known

But I've got to rearrange
I like to keep it strange
I like to feel the change...
When it rains...

I've got to rearrange
I like to keep it strange
I like to feel the change...
When it rains...

"The only way to make sense out of change is to plunge into it,
move with it, and join the dance."

—ALAN WATTS

"This songs kicks ass!" was the first public feedback I received on "Sail Away." The remark came from an older gentleman in the audience who hadn't said much all evening. Upon hearing this song, however, he was suddenly on his feet dancing up a storm. It is nice to receive this kind of validation, but it's even cooler to see the healing power of my music in action. When I finished playing, I chatted briefly with the man, and he affirmed something I had always felt was true.

"There's so much crappy music I hear on the radio these days, but man, you got the spirit of rock and roll in you!" he said, adding, "I never hear music with good riffs anymore, the kind that get stuck in your head and keep ya groovin' out all day!"

I was thrilled to have blessed this man's eardrums with a riff that could help him achieve and maintain a groovy attitude.

While many of my songs are acoustic with a calm and relaxed feel, this one is pure rock and roll. In fact, it was the first song I ever wrote on an electric guitar. While listening, the opening riff can be heard repeated over and over during the verses. The repetition of this riff generally leads people in the audience at my shows to begin tapping their feet and bobbing their heads within seconds of me playing. Why is this?

The answer is simple. Repetition in music is pleasing to our ears. Amid all of life's uncertainty, there is something extremely comforting about knowing what's going to happen next. This song is about change, but it incorporates repetition in order to hook the listener and get the message across. To illustrate this phenomenon more deeply, I've included an excerpt from one of my favorite books, *This Is Your Brain on Music* by Daniel J. Levitin.

"Music is based on repetition. Music works because we remember the tones we had just heard and are relating them to the ones that are just now being played. Those groups of tones— phrases—might come up later in the piece in a variation that tickles our memory system at the same time as it activates our emotional centers... Repetition, when done skillfully by a master composer, is emotionally satisfying to our brains, and makes the listening experience as pleasurable as it is."
—THIS IS YOUR BRAIN ON MUSIC, BY DANIEL J. LEVITIN.

Considering this profound effect repetition has on our emotions, it's easy to see why certain songs become instant hits. I did not write this song with that intention, but I immediately felt the satisfaction that came from repeatedly playing the riff.

If a piece of music is inspiring positive feelings within me, I usually keep playing it because there's a good chance it will then inspire positive words. This method is how many songs of mine end up being written. With this particular song, I had the riff long before the lyrics. I would play it while jamming with my dad on the drums, and pretty soon we had it nailed down and sounding tight.

A few months later, the right words fell into place without much effort. I had just gone through an abrupt breakup with a girl I was crazy about and was left without any real closure. I wanted that closure so I could move on. I felt I needed insight and genuine reasons for why this happened beyond what my worrying mind came up with. It was very difficult for me to move past it without an explanation. One day I was feeling particularly sad about the situation and decided to play guitar to take my mind off it. Since this song's riff always gave me a feeling of empowerment, I decided to play it. Within minutes, the words began to flow, and I instantly understood what my soul was expressing to me through the music. The lyrics reflect my state of mind once I finally realized I needed to accept the situation and move forward with my life.

WHAT IS CHANGE?

Change is an essential part of our lives and of nature itself. In fact, the only constant in life is change. But change is merely a word, and quite frankly, it doesn't do a phenomenal job of describing the way situations unfold and develop. Flow would be a much better word for describing the human perspective on how we evolve as individual beings over time. You see, change implies that one thing becomes another. In a sense, this is true. But a "thing" is finite. So, to say one "thing" becomes another "thing" is not fully accurate. What's really going on is that energy is shifting forms, flowing from one state to the next.

A perfect analogy to illustrate this idea lies in the most foundational element of our existence: the very breath in our lungs. A breath is not a thing—it is a process of energy flowing back and forth. When we refuse to embrace change, we are trying to hold onto the present moment in a way that disempowers us. It is like trying to savor life by holding our breath. All we end up doing is blocking the flow of fresh, new energy to us. If we learn to embrace the changes in our lives, we can then learn to operate in harmony with nature, instead of opposing it.

With this new awareness, we open ourselves up to the realization that the present moment is always here, and we do not need to hold onto it in order to enjoy it. Acceptance of this fact can be a hard lesson to learn, but it is the only way we can move forward in life. Many wonderful new experiences await us in the future, but we cannot experience them unless we learn how to live in the moment. If we don't, then we will also not be fully present in the future when those new blessings and opportunities greet us, and we will miss them.

"Without remaining open to change, we cannot remain open to life."

—RAM DASS

CAN'T BE WRONG

———

All this wasted time,
And all these wasted lines
They paint a picture, of you

Take away my pride,
nowhere left to hide,
it's my commitment, to you

And now I know it can't be wrong,
To sing my song
Now you know it can't be wrong,
To sing your song

All that's said and done,
Makes me want to run
Far away from here, and all your fear

And now I know it can't be wrong,
to sing my song
now you know it can't be wrong,
to sing your song

"Re-examine all you have been told at school or church or in any book, dismiss whatever insults your own soul; and your very flesh shall be a great poem, and have the richest fluency, not only in its words, but in the silent lines of its lips and face, and between the lashes of your eyes, and in every motion and joint of your body.

—WALT WHITMAN

Imposter syndrome. Maybe you've heard of it, maybe you've even experienced it. I know I certainly have. It is the feeling of being unqualified to do the work you do. Most commonly, it manifests as a feeling of inner doubt or insecurity about our skills, accompanied by a fear of being exposed as some sort of fraud. Despite evidence of our creative abilities, we find it hard to give ourselves the credit we deserve. Why is this phenomenon so common?

As children, we are taught that we do not have authority. We are taught to obey the commands of our parents, teachers, older siblings, and chaperones. We grow up believing we need to ask for permission to do what we want to do. But when a child is allowed to play, our innate human creativity shines brightly for all to see. So, where does it go? As we grow up and start attempting to succeed in a complex society, many of us lose that creative spark. It gets lost as we try to fit in and seek acceptance. We try to *impress* instead of *express*, and when we do that, we are not singing our song.

In life, we encounter great learning, great loss, and great triumphs, but what is most important to our happiness and contentment is our expression. I'm talking about the expression and evolution of the soul—my soul, your soul, our soul. Soul energy is the most brilliant radiant light in all the many universes. It is pure conscious being, too comprehensive for any one person to understand upon beholding it. It is a concept so massive and benevolent that failure is impossible within its parameters, which are no parameters, and thus the notion of failure, being predicated upon achieving some definable end goal, is rendered meaningless.

Still, there is capacity for suffering and perceived tragedy here on Earth, and it is the duty of the artist to transform the suffering of those who cannot see a way out. The artist must gather the courage to harness and implement the innate gifts and talents they possess in order to inspire hope, change, and belief in the positive and righteous aspects of life. Through music, storytelling, film, painting, poetry, literature, dance, design, athletics, comedy, the artist loses and abandons individual personhood to become the art itself. Art allows the artist to speak to the audience in a deeper way, with less formality and less judgment. Most importantly, art is subjective. Even when art is intentional, there is still room for people to interpret a creative work in the way that makes sense to them, without fear of being wrong.

This is what makes art so powerful: It has no end goal, no necessary outcome. It cannot succeed or fail because it is simply an expression of life. Mindful art and music can open us up to the bliss that exists in the present moment, allowing us the opportunity to experience genuine delight via our senses.

"There is something in every one of you that waits and listens for the sound of the genuine in yourself. It is the only true

guide you will ever have, and if you cannot hear it, you will all of your life spend your days on the ends of strings that somebody else pulls."

—HOWARD THURMAN

Is it possible for us to look at ourselves, at human life, the same way we look at art? Are we not as imperfectly beautiful as the *Mona Lisa* or the *Statue of David*? I believe we are. I believe there can be no wrong way to be yourself. We all have inherent value as individuals because we each have a purely unique perspective to offer the world. I cannot see through your eyes, and you cannot hear with my ears. We each represent the possibilities and potential of the universe in our own way.

SING YOUR SONG

I will never forget the day I received the phone call that my song "Safe as We Can" had made the ballot for the GRAM-MYs. Not only was it thrilling, but it was almost hard to believe. I kept thinking, *Who am I to be competing against Paul McCartney, Blink 182, and The Black Keys?* Well, the answer was simple. I am me, and I always will be. Just like those artists didn't get to where they are by trying to be some-body else, all I need to do is embrace who I am and create with confidence. I have a story to tell that is just as valid as anyone else's.

Still, there were so many limiting beliefs I held onto from my past. When I started performing as a professional musi-cian, it was incredibly difficult to overcome the imposter syndrome—at first. But the more times I saw my name up in lights, or received compliments and praise from audiences, the more I realized I was doing exactly what I was born to do. I am so incredibly grateful to be able to play music for a living. It gives me a chance to interact with other people and heal them with my positive loving energy. Even when people are unsupportive and hurtful, I remind myself those are the people who need love the most.

Sometimes people try to drag each other down. They may do this on purpose or by accident, consciously or subconsciously. But it's important to remember that while others do have the power to influence you, you have the power to walk away from influences you deem unfit for your growth and happiness. It is your responsibility alone to figure out who is truly supporting you and who is not!

"There's an African proverb: 'When death finds you, may it find you alive.' Alive means living your own damned life, not the life that your parents wanted, or the life some cultural group or political party wanted, but the life that your own soul wants to live."

—MICHAEL MEADE

There will always be people who try to discourage you from pursuing your dreams. This is because a more actualized version of you requires a more actualized version of them to keep pace, and people are deeply afraid of and doubt their own abilities. When someone tells you something you want is crazy, or that your ideas or plans to be great or successful at something are crazy or unrealistic, just remember: what they're really saying is "Who do you think you are?" And when you actually know who you are, the hard part is already over. Faith in oneself is step one. Faith in the world is not necessary. You can't always rely on external conditions to support your endeavors. The determination and will to create must come from within! So don't be afraid to sing your song, because it can't be wrong!

"Things are as they are. Looking out into the universe at night, we make no comparisons between right and wrong stars, nor between well and badly arranged constellations."
— ALAN WATTS

KEEP IT AT BAY

If you wanna make change in the world today
You gotta talk to people, every day
You gotta walk with people, and show 'em the way
You gotta stop the evil, keep it at bay

If you wanna spread peace in the world today
You gotta watch the thoughts that eat you away
You gotta stop the feelings that lead you astray
Outsmart your ego, keep it at bay

Keep it at bay, yeah

If you wanna succeed in the world today
You gotta speak the truth that's hidden away
You gotta let 'em know you got somethin' to say
Show heart to ego, keep it at bay

Keep it at bay, yeah

You can't start a fire when you're feelin' sad
Sometimes life is gonna drive you mad

Take a deep breath, it'll be okay
Cuz they're gonna love you anyway
You just gotta learn to keep it at bay

Keep it at bay, yeah
Keep it at bay, yeah

"The quality of our life depends on the quality of the seeds that lie deep in our consciousness."

—THICH NHAT HANH

Each time you repeat a thought to yourself, you are planting a seed. But a seed alone cannot grow. It needs to be watered regularly. The seeds in our minds are watered by the people we hang out with, the music we listen to, the art we experience, and the foods we eat. But most importantly, they are watered by the words we speak to ourselves. Positive seeds, when watered with compassion and insight, grow into positive feelings, which lead to beautiful actions. It's as simple as that. These actions create a ripple effect, ultimately leading to a more compassionate society. When we look at this phenomenon through the lens of music, we can easily see that positive, mindful, and uplifting songs inspire us to create more love in our lives. The best part? These songs provide us a chance to share that love with others!

I believe something fundamental about art and music: When created and used mindfully, art and music can transform a society. In fact, art *does* transform societies. Each day, millions of mindful artists and musicians are expressing their love, understanding, vulnerability, fears, desires, and so much more. This kind of art requires empathy, and empathy empowers our society to understand each other's needs and our own on a deeper level. This in turn fosters not only positive growth and community, but the development of new tools for shaping our reality. Whether those tools are material or psychological, we evolve as a species either way. Creating music, specifically, is so powerful because it requires us to listen in to the collective story of humanity and come up with a new perspective on the story.

Playing music requires me to empathize, to listen deeply, and to contribute to the best of my abilities what I feel is appropriate in any musical situation. Music teaches me when to speak, and when to be silent. I know I have gifts to bestow upon others. So many people, from strangers and fans to family and friends, have told me I've changed their lives, and that I've inspired them to be happy about who they are or to change what they don't like about their lives. Perhaps this is because I live my life in an authentic way and try my best not to let the opinions of others define who I am becoming. That's what success looks like to me: being unapologetic for living the life you've always imagined for yourself!

As an artist, I don't necessarily wish for the public to become consumers of my art and music, but rather to become consumers of the message my words are speaking.

Music allows us to take language and give it multiple meanings. The words are suggestions toward feelings, which are the only real thing we experience. You can't experience a word. You can experience a feeling and then use words to attempt to describe what you're feeling, but you cannot locate or define a word because words are intangible. Words are the names we use to point toward feelings and concepts. And you cannot experience a concept any more than you can experience a word. For example, we know oxytocin is the chemical responsible for feelings of love, but the word oxytocin is not love, and the word oxytocin cannot make us feel love. Life itself is state of feeling, and our thoughts come directly from experiencing a particular feeling or combination of feelings.

All this to say, we create meaning in our lives based on how we feel, but we do it by using words. It's so easy to get sucked into the hallucination of life in modern society. Human culture can be so distracting that we forget we are actually animals with a *lot* of material comforts. Many material comforts offer us freedom from the toils of hard labor, but other inventions allow us to construct new realities altogether.

For example, the pen I first used to write these words is more than a material comfort. It is a tool, an instrument used to evoke meaning from nature. We literally write our reality into existence. From the first letter to the first word, to the first story ever written, we shape our reality using words. What we think about and focus on, we create more of. If we are constantly feeding our minds with negative thoughts and words, we cannot have a positive life. But with mindfulness and compassion, we can use this power to create an abundance of joy and happiness in our lives.

BUILDING YOUR IDEAL REALITY

My friendship with my cousin Alex is a shining example of the positive results that come from implementing this simple principle of shaping our reality with our thoughts and words. He and I worked for years to surround ourselves with positive, optimistic, and encouraging people. We are both extremely loyal to friends and family, a trait that, as many of us know, can make it hard to break away from negative energy or people we are close with. But doing so has worked profound miracles in both of our lives.

Whenever Alex and I hung out, we would vent to each other about the difficult or annoying things in our lives. It was a way of bonding through acknowledging each other's struggles. But in 2016, I started practicing aspects of mindfulness I had learned at Blue Cliff and integrating them into my life. Alex noticed my energy becoming more and more positive over time. Instead of wasting energy talking about the people who'd wronged us, we decided to use our time together to build each other up. Alex has always encouraged me and believed in my inevitable success as a musician. He would say things to me like, "You're already successful, man, because you've got the right attitude toward life."

Soon, we began using the principles of this simple law of attraction to manifest wonderful things into our lives. Before all this, Alex and I were both single, living at home with our parents, and working part-time jobs. Alex knew he didn't want to go to a traditional college, but he hadn't quite figured out a plan or discovered his passion. I had graduated college with a bachelor's degree in marketing but found every job I applied for in the business world to be terribly unfulfilling.

We started working together on a mutual vision for our futures and decided we wanted to get a place together once we could afford it.

About a year later, I was finally able to buy a house and made it work by renting out a room to Alex and my other friend, Dave. Our dream of living together had come true! We then got to see each other almost every day, which made it easier and easier to help each other stay positive and provide encouragement. Around the same time, Alex graduated from New England Tech and landed a job working for a local electrician. Not two weeks later, he met the love of his life, Kiana. She is a wonderful person who has overcome a lot of adversity but always has a positive outlook and expresses her gratitude for each day. I was thrilled to see my cousin so happy and fulfilled.

In May of 2020, Alex and Kiana welcomed their beautiful daughter Holly into this world. On top of that, they bought their first home and adopted an adorable husky named Luna. Alex is still working as a professional electrician's apprentice and is about to earn his own license to practice. He and I have been on a whirlwind ride of exciting life transformations that have resulted in us both getting everything we've ever wanted. Even better, we did it by following our hearts and keeping our minds clear of negative debris. The value of this practice cannot be understated!

THE UNIVERSE IS LISTENING
The universe listens and responds to our thoughts, and we will attract into our lives what we fill our minds with. Here

is a phrase I wrote in my journal one morning that I repeat often to keep myself on track:

"I am keeping my thoughts pure and my heart open in order to experience the flow of positive energy I am always attracting."

Notice the language includes "I am," and the verbs are in the present tense. This drills the message into the subconscious mind because I am affirming this sentence as a state of continuous doing and being. Every vibration you experience, whether positive or negative, contributes a piece to the mosaic of who you are. If we practice patience and use compassionate words with ourselves and others, we will keep the darkness at bay. Then, we can create art and music from a place of deep positive intention and communicate the ineffable truths we hold in our hearts. We can learn to first see, and then express the positive light in every situation.

"Every cell is eavesdropping on your internal dialogue."
                                                    —DEEPAK CHOPRA

NEW YORK MAN

———

Saw some things I had never seen
Goin' after my favorite dream
Shakin' hands with celebrity fans
New York man, got no plans

I have found somethin' bigger than me
Queen of time, yeah she rests with me
Makin' friends and abandonin' trends
New York man, got no plans

Apathy is my enemy
I see what I want to see
Drivin' fast, cuz we're makin' it last
New York man, got no plans

Makin' friends and abandonin' trends
New York man, got no plans
New York man, got no plans

"You will never do anything in this world without courage. It is the greatest quality of the mind next to honor."

—ARISTOTLE

There I was, twenty-four years old, in a room of ten to fifteen men and about three hundred women. We were all waiting for one extremely badass woman to take the stage. It's not often you get to save the day for one of your heroes, who also happens to be a celebrity. This particular heroine was professional life/business coach and *New York Times* best-selling author Jen Sincero. Jen had been living in a small one-car garage before her first book, *You Are a Badass*, became a best-seller. The subtitle of the book was *to stop doubting your greatness and live an awesome life.*

The event was being held at The Guild, a huge brewery with fifty-foot ceilings and large beer tanks that were making a constant hum in the background. Using an app on my phone, I detected about seventy-five decibels of ambient noise in the room. This is the equivalent of being in a car driving on the highway, so as you can imagine, it was already hard to hear. The introduction began, and as I expected, people were having trouble making out the words. To make matters worse, the microphone and speaker were making extremely loud and irksome high-pitched noises. I'm talking about that shrill, nails-on-a-chalkboard sound that makes you want to crawl out of your skin. The audience members were growing restless, and you could hear the groans of discomfort echoing throughout the large room.

Robin, the woman running the event, finished her introduction and announced that Jen would be on stage in just a few minutes. When she put the microphone down, it made one final awful sound before chatter filled the room as we all waited eagerly for Jen to come out from backstage.

I desperately wanted to at least attempt to fix the microphone, but I wasn't sure if it was a good idea. There were several hundred already disgruntled people waiting for Jen to speak. I was afraid of looking foolish with all those eyes on me, but I knew this was my chance to act. I knew if I didn't act, no one else would. I also knew the window of time to act would be very small. The success of the event was compromised, and I possessed the knowledge to solve the problem.

So, despite my fear, I took action. I stood up, glanced to my right, and asked the group of young ladies seated next to me to please allow me to squeeze by them and exit the row.

"Where are you going?" one of the girls asked. "Jen's about to speak!"

I turned back and gave her a look of conviction. "Not yet she's not!" I said.

As I walked down the center aisle, the stares came just as I had expected. I shook them off and remained focused. Assessing the problem during my approach, I could see things weren't looking good. There was only one small speaker about the size of a ukulele being used to try and fill the enormous room. I could still feel everyone's stares, but it was too late to turn back now. I walked right onto the stage and tapped Robin on the shoulder.

"Excuse me," I said quietly. "I apologize for coming on stage without asking, but I'm a professional musician and experienced sound engineer. I really think I could help make the speaker sound better and stop making those feedback noises."

A look of relief washed over her face instantly as she processed my words.

"Oh my gosh, thank you so much," she said graciously. "That would be a big help because I have no idea how to work this thing!"

"Great!" I exclaimed, excited she was receptive to my help.

I started by showing her the most important step for clear audio, which is to speak directly into the microphone, holding it like you would a megaphone rather than holding it vertically below your chin.

"This allows the soundwaves from your voice to travel directly into the mic instead of floating over the top," I said, while quickly demonstrating.

"Step two," I said, "is to never point the mic toward the speaker itself. That's what causes the feedback noise. Keeping your body in between them also helps to prevent that noise."

The improvement was immediately noticeable when she tested the sound by saying:

"Thank you to this kind gentleman for volunteering to help us fix the sound issue!"

I felt venerated and confident as the audience cheered and clapped.

Next, I walked over to the speaker itself to examine the volume and tone settings. As I suspected, the high-end frequency was turned way up, and the low-end frequency was turned way down. As a general rule, a woman's voice occupies a higher frequency range than a man's voice, so I put the knobs in a more balanced position to boost the bass volume slightly while reducing the treble. I then nodded for Robin to test the mic once more.

"Testing, testing!" she said.

Again, the sound had noticeably improved. Once the sound was balanced in that way, I was able to turn up the master volume without any feedback problems whatsoever. As I was turning the final knob, I caught the feeling of someone looking at me from my periphery. To my delight, it was none other than Jen Sincero herself, holding the microphone, waiting for *me* to give *her* the okay to start speaking.

"*Thank you!*" she whispered to me with a big smile on her face.

"No, thank *you!*" I said. "I wouldn't have had the courage to come up here if I hadn't remembered I was a badass!"

She laughed, and we shook hands before I got down from the stage and returned to my seat while applause filled the room. The applause was for Jen, but I knew it was partly for me, too.

In that moment, I realized I had just done exactly what Jen's book title suggested. I overcame my fear, trusted my greatness, and saved the day like the badass I am.

The talk went swimmingly, and everyone could hear Jen's words clearly. She spoke about having the courage to take the leap of faith and go for your dreams, something I was actively doing as a professional musician. Her writing in the first *Badass* book was honest, vulnerable, captivating, and direct. But oddly enough, she hadn't yet experienced the success she was writing about. She wanted more for herself in life, but her relationship with money had always been self-defeating and pessimistic. "I'll always be broke," she used to tell herself. "I don't deserve to be rich." I used to personally identify with these sentiments, until I read her second book *You are a Badass at Making Money.*

Jen's book changed not only my perspective on money, but my relationship with my own self-worth, and my own value. She redefined what the term "rich" meant, saying that being rich means "to be able to afford all of the things and experiences required to fully live your most authentic life." I knew I was deserving of the level of wealth that would allow me to live that kind of life, but the amount was still unclear to me. As a professional musician, I was already getting paid to do what I loved, and I felt grateful to be getting paid at all. But after reading that book and hearing her speak, I realized there was room for me to make much more money playing music than I ever thought possible.

Jen helped me to see that I was indeed deserving of riches, in the sense of having the resources to be able to spread my music across the globe without worrying about how I was going to pay the bills. I started to recognize my worth on a deeper level. If I really believed the music I was playing and creating had value, then I knew it was right for me to have the financial means to share that value on a larger scale.

Jen's wisdom helped me create a new paradigm for myself and my music. That night was April 24, 2018. Being freshly equipped with my new money-positive attitude, I had a much more lucrative summer playing music than in previous years. I was even able to buy my first home that September! The best part is I didn't have to worry about how I was going to pay the mortgage because believing in myself and my art had almost doubled my income!

According to Jen Sincero, you have to truly believe you really can have what you desire, that it already exists, and then go out and get it. I have since broken into the private event market for music and began playing weddings, birthday parties, corporate events, fundraisers, and other higher paying gigs. These opportunities had always existed around me, but I had to value myself and my gifts enough to make them a reality.

I'll never forget the day I played a wedding and made more than double what my weekly salary had been working full-time. I also got a generous tip for doing such a good job. The best part is the clients were eager to pay me this much money because of the immense amount of value I provided for them. I made their events infinitely more engaged and memorable with the good vibrations and positive energy of my music!

THE MAKINGS OF A SONG

Sometimes, you write a song and you have no idea what it even means. You just know the words feel right and the music is flowing. Some of the lyrics might not make sense at all until months or even years later. Both were the case for this particular song. But as certain things came to pass in my life, the hidden messages began to reveal themselves. On some level, a certain part of me must have known what I was trying to say with these lyrics, but the song was completely vague when I first wrote it. All I know is it gave me the right feeling. Sometimes, that's all that matters. Some of the best songs are ones that were never intended to be written. In fact, "New York Man" only came to exist because of a conversation I had with my Auntie Pat.

I had just returned from a weekend in New York City visiting my friend Nataliya, a global fashion sustainability consultant I met at Blue Cliff Monastery. On the way back home, I stopped to see my cousin Alex. As I mentioned earlier in the book, we are more like brothers than cousins, always encouraging each other to strive for more in life and grow as individuals. Alex's younger brother Eric had just gotten a guitar for Christmas, and I was messing around experimenting with some new chords. After a few minutes, my Auntie Pat came into the room and said, "Ayyy, New York man!" We all laughed, and Alex said, "That sounds like a cool song title!" Naturally, I took this as a challenge to write a cool enough song to match the title. A few weeks later, I had the makings of a song on my hands!

BEING A BADASS AT LIFE

I don't have to have a boss or work for a company anymore because I get paid to play my guitar and sing for people. That's pretty incredible. In fact, it's a miracle! I am so grateful to be able to put positive vibrations out into the world in exchange for the money and resources necessary to support myself and create more beautiful art and music. I believe everyone can achieve this freedom to some degree. We all have such unique gifts to offer, but often we are too busy following the norm or status quo. We are fearful of new ways of existing outside our comfort zone. But the funny thing is, the more you practice doing things that are scary or outside your comfort zone, the more your comfort zone expands. I've learned some very valuable lessons in the pursuit of my dreams as a career, but this one is by far the most important:

Fear is the only thing that gets smaller as you run toward it.

People have told me, "Wow, I wish I had your life," because they see an outer image of a lifestyle they like or idolize. But what they don't see is everything I've done behind the scenes to make this lifestyle possible. I do many things differently than most people. No one else can be me because they are too busy being themselves. That sentence has multiple different meanings as we examine it more closely. People are so busy being themselves that they can't see the underlying motives for their own behavior. If they could, we might say, "Hey look, what you're really after is x, but your behavior is y because it makes you think and feel like you're getting x." Many people want to pursue their dreams, but they are too busy being themselves and doing what they already do. They begin to associate those behaviors with who they are.

If you want to be the person whose dreams become realities, you have to start making new choices and doing things you've never done before.

You must work one on one with the universe to bring forth your creation into existence, into reality. The very fact that we *can* bring something new into existence proves just how much creative power we have.

The core aspect of reality is that it is malleable; it can be readily changed by our actions at any moment.

When you eat an apple instead of a candy bar, you are creating a healthier world by setting an example and choosing nutrients over nonsense. When you take actions that bring you closer to your dreams instead of continuing your old habits, you are making the world a slightly happier place by being truer to yourself, and again setting an example for others to be happier!

If you see yourself as a struggling artist, it's time to start abandoning the trends of your own limiting beliefs and behaviors, as well as your identification with broke starving artist stereotypes. It may be scary at first, but you will undoubtedly find the strength you need to push past fear by trusting your gifts and your greatness.

"We must have courage to bet on our ideas, to take the calculated risk, and to act. Everyday living requires courage if life is to be effective and bring happiness."
—MAXWELL MALTZ

MAPLE LEAF

I am a maple leaf, dancing in the wind
I am the raindrop, cleansing my skin
I am a snowflake, taking a shape I've never seen
I am all these things colliding in a dream
I am all these things colliding, in a dream

I am the sunshine, lighting up my days
I am the bluebird, singing my praise
I am a servant, like the mighty evergreen
I am all these things colliding in a dream
I am all these things colliding, in a dream

I am a mountain, reaching for the sky
I am a falcon, flying so high
An energetic river, rushing gently down the stream
I am all these things, colliding in a dream
I am all these things colliding in a dream

I am a spider, weaving the web of inter-being,
I am all these things, colliding in a dream

I am a seeker, wondering, what it all could mean...
I am all these things, colliding in a dream
I am all these things, colliding in a dream
We are all these things, colliding...
In a dream

"I believe a leaf of grass is no less than the journey-work of the stars."

—WALT WHITMAN

When I was eight years old, I really wanted to change my name to Walker Texas Ranger. After finding out you can legally change your name once you turn sixteen, I was overjoyed. I didn't really like my name all that much, and if Walker Texas Ranger was an option, I was taking it. I mean... Nathan Jones? Nathan Steven Jones? Looking back, I probably just didn't like my name because I didn't like my life or didn't like school and the way I was treated by the other kids. My name didn't represent something positive to me. Needless to say, I never ended up changing my name... But I did get a new one.

In October of 2016, I attended my third mindfulness retreat. It was hosted by some members of the New England sangha at a retreat center in Maine. While there, I met two former monks who had fallen in love at Plum Village Monastery in France. Their names were Michael and Fern, and they run a mindful living community and retreat center in New Hampshire called Morning Sun. On the final day of the retreat, Michael bestowed me with a Dharma name. Dharma means "truth/teaching," and I was receiving this name as part of a transmission of the Five Mindfulness Trainings created by Thich Nhat Hanh. The Dharma name is selected based on observations of the recipient's personality and character. It is used as a means of instilling a deeper connection to the practice of mindfulness. So, what was this new name of mine, you ask? Well, it's one of the most badass names I've ever heard:

"Energetic River of the Source."

But wait, how did we get here?

On a warm, breezy summer night in 2018, I was relaxing on the couch playing my guitar, experimenting with different chords. I had just finished some gratitude journaling and was reflecting on all the blessings in my life. I was in exactly the right state of mind to harness the flow of music pouring out of me. I recall looking up and seeing a picture of my five-year-old self on the mantle of the fireplace. The photo was in a golden, sunflower-shaped frame which cast a shadow on the wall behind it resembling that of a maple leaf. Upon noticing this, I jokingly said to myself, "I'm a maple leaf!" Because I was still playing the guitar, I said it softly, in an almost whispering voice. *That actually sounded nice*, I thought to myself.

Realizing I was onto something, I kept singing and playing the altered D chord I was fretting on the guitar. Before I knew it, I had the beginning of a song. The entire process was so natural. In that moment, I knew I was merely the vessel through which the song was being channeled. The message coming through was one of unity, inter-being, and shifted perspectives.

INTER-BEING

One day during my senior year of high school, my English teacher Ms. Mizer was absent, so she assigned our class a creative writing exercise. The prompt instructed us to write for twenty minutes and describe ourselves using non-human characteristics. At first, I found the exercise challenging. I didn't know where to begin. But once the first line popped into my head, the rest of the words began to flow. This is what I came up with:

I am the world.

I am a ray of sunshine in an otherwise dark sky. No one can hide in the darkness, for it is cancelled out by my light. I am a mirage in the middle of the desert. Many will reach out to touch me, but alas, I am not truly there. I am an island in the sea. The waves crash over me, but there I remain. I am a grassy meadow in a dark forest. Those passing through will stop to rest in my clover-covered pastures. I am a mountain reaching up toward the heavens in stark contrast to the surrounding plains. No man can reach my summit, for my sides are simply too steep to scale.

I am an iceberg floating in the ocean; most of me is under the surface. Those who judge me have not seen my entirety. I am a shady tree in the savanna. My sprawling canopy provides refuge for weary travelers. I am a majestic stallion roaming freely through the grassland. No one can tame the wild beast inside of me. I am the omniscient eye of an eagle. Observant and sharp, nothing can evade my attention. I am a pond frozen over. Those who try to cross me may taste my icy revenge.

I am an avalanche in the mountains. No object can stand in my way. Nothing can deter me.

I am the world—and the world is what I make of it.

I definitely shocked myself that day with how cool this piece of writing turned out. As it was coming together, I sensed a clear theme and stuck with it. I was very proud of the final result. In fact, I even used it as my college essay! Looking back on this essay after writing "Maple Leaf," I noticed many similarities. It was clear I had always enjoyed drawing parallels between my own human nature and the nature of the world around me. I believed strongly that the world was what I made of it. In the seven years between writing this essay and writing "Maple Leaf," several key experiences showed me how many of these metaphysical ideas are actually true.

The concept of inter-being is about awareness and realization of the interconnected nature of the entire universe. We live our lives through the lens of the ego, which functions by creating boundaries from the world around it. Things like music, meditation, and certain plant medicines help dissolve some of those boundaries between the perceived self and the environment. I know my identity as a person named Nate Jones is merely an illusion. I am pure electromagnetic energy, vibrating and manifesting itself in a unique and highly complex disguise in order to experience an individual perspective.

The atoms comprising my body are no different than the atoms comprising a maple leaf, a raindrop, or a snowflake. The energy allowing my body to form and grow is no different than the energy that creates a mountain or a river.

My brain runs on the same electricity powering the brain of the bluebird or the falcon. When I came up with the line about all these things colliding in a dream, a shot of pure ecstasy coursed through my body. It was a moment of deep awareness and philosophical understanding, created through music. It was a demonstration of the exact kind of power I'm talking about, creating a physical sensation in my body as a result of picking up an instrument and letting words flow. The vibrations created a chemical reaction which produced a physical feeling in me as a direct result of my playing and singing.

But let's get back to the story of my Dharma name.

At twenty-three years old, I had just started playing music professionally and was still finding my way in my new career. The music industry can at times be very toxic and difficult to navigate. Being at bars night after night presented me with many temptations. I was offered free drinks at every single show, and it was difficult to say no because I wanted to be polite and sociable. After just a few months of performing, I was already beginning to see how I was adopting unhealthy habits that limited my growth.

After receiving my Dharma name, I made the commitment to stop drinking alcohol at my shows. I found that alcohol disconnected me from my heart and my true feelings and showed me a distorted view of reality. Now, whenever someone offered to buy me a drink, I would just tell them I don't drink but I appreciate their gesture very much. I noticed immediate improvements in my presence, energy, and endurance at my shows. This state of focus and flow helped me to intuitively merge with everything around me and become one with my environment. I was seeing clearly and reading the room from moment to moment to decide what songs to play.

Whenever I was faced with the temptation to drink, I repeated my Dharma name to myself. It reminded me that I already possessed everything I needed to channel the music from my heart. Even during tough moments, I knew it was better to connect with my emotions rather than subdue them. Some of the best songs ever written were born from extreme pain and sorrow over the hardships we endure in life. I was able to have a good time without drinking by surrendering to the flow of the music and losing touch with my ego in the process. I reminded myself that even though I was playing, I was technically at work. With this awareness, the commitment to providing entertainment for others through the songs became my higher purpose. I felt my heart open wider as my love and understanding grew with each performance.

I wrote the final lyrics of "Maple Leaf" in the monk's office of the meditation hall at Blue Cliff Monastery just minutes before performing it for one hundred fifty people at a retreat. One of the most important lessons I've ever learned came right after performing this song. Several people had walked up to me to thank me for playing and sharing my music. I talked about how rewarding it was to be able to play for such an engaged, tuned-in audience compared to playing out at a bar. After some discussion with the group, someone caught me off guard, saying, "But think about it, Nate. Those people drinking at the bar are the ones who need your music and good vibes the most."

Not once had this thought crossed my mind, because I was still learning that my shows were not about me and my feelings or preferences, but about what I can give to the audience. I came to a deeper understanding of my role as a musician. I realized so many of the people out drinking were looking for something, searching for happiness, just trying to relax and have a good time. What if my presence could make the difference between someone having a good day or a bad day?

Maybe, I thought to myself, *the musical medicine I'm providing will be stronger than what they're getting at the bar.*

I then started treating my shows as opportunities to create healing in public. In reality, I merely came to the realization I had been doing this all along. I just couldn't see it until I expanded my awareness through the practice of mindfulness. Just because I was at a bar didn't mean my performances were only about entertainment. They were also about bringing people together to experience healing. Acknowledging how my healing is connected to the healing of others through music was the first step in my journey toward living out the meaning of my Dharma name. This is where the concept of inter-being comes back into play. When I perform, I am acting as a vessel, channeling the healing and empowering energy of music through my own body and into the consciousness of those around me.

"We are here to awaken from our illusion of separateness."

—THICH NHAT HANH

HOLD THE KNIFE

———

How many more times, will we see them bled?
How many more times. will we dye them red?
How many more times, 'til you see the thread?
How many more times, 'til it's you who's dead?

But just one time, will you hold the knife?
Just one time, will you hold the knife?

Will you take a life?
Will you hold the knife?

How many more times, will you watch them die?
How many more times, will you call them swine?
How many more times, will you close your eyes?
How many more times, will they pay the price?

But just one time, will you hold the knife?
I said just one time, will you hold the knife?

Will you take a life?
Will you hold the knife?

Will you hold the knife?

Just one time—will you hold the knife?

"The greatness of a nation and its moral progress can be judged by the way its animals are treated."

—GANDHI

Standing no more than ten feet apart, our eyes were locked in on each other's. A warm, delighted smile began to stretch across my face. She was so beautiful. I could tell she trusted me, otherwise this encounter would not be happening. Looking more closely, I realized she only had three legs... I had never dreamed I would be able to get this close to a mother deer and her babies!

It was a warm and sunny fall afternoon, and I was walking alone through the forest on the last day of the creative arts retreat at Blue Cliff Monastery. It was also my mother's birthday, the twenty-fifth of September. Little did I know, this precious moment would forever influence the way I live my life.

I saw something in that deer's eyes, something beautiful—something like myself. I had been meditating that morning on my mother's love and was excited to drive home to see her on her birthday. I thought of all the times she protected me, stood up for me, how I knew she would give her life for me in an instant without hesitation. When I gazed into this deer's eyes, I saw my mother's love. I saw how similar we are as creatures. It was absolute bliss. She was trusting me to be extremely close to her babies, knowing I had absolutely zero intention of causing her harm in any way.

I have always loved animals. I love playing with them, watching them do silly things, and sharing videos of adorable animals online. Unfortunately, I have also seen videos online of animals being treated in a manner I can only describe as evil. I've always known that if I ever came across someone abusing an animal, I would put a stop to it immediately and even risk my life in doing so. In that moment with the deer, I realized that every single day of my life, my actions *did* cause animals harm.

Every single time I bought a hamburger, or ate ice cream, pizza, or scrambled some eggs from the store, I was supporting animal abuse with my dollar. I was paying someone else to do to an animal what I would never dream of doing and could not be paid any amount of money to do. Animal abuse for no reason is bad enough, but I was participating in animal abuse for a *profit*. I felt sick to my stomach. How could I have been so blind to my own actions?

In that moment, I knew there would be no possible way I would ever eat the flesh of a living being again. I felt a deep sense of compassion wash over me as that thought became my new reality. I continued to stare at this beautiful, intelligent, living, breathing being eating some lunch and protecting her children while they played nearby. We are both animals, and despite our differences, we are both capable of experiencing suffering.

When a moral and ethical injustice is taking place over and over again, it is the duty of those who can do something about it to speak out and act as advocates to put a stop to it.

WHAT DOES IT MEAN TO LOVE ANIMALS?

There is a festival every year in Yulin, China, where thousands of dogs are slaughtered to be cooked and eaten. I have seen many people who are outraged by this, even going so far as to call the perpetrators "barbarians." Somehow, these same people do not feel any remorse about eating dead animals for whom they paid to be abused and slaughtered. Are they not also "barbarians" for doing it to a cow or pig instead of a dog?

I understand many people hunt for survival, and I respect that need. There is nothing wrong with people eating animals when there are no other food options. So long as the animal is not being tortured first, hunting out of pure necessity can be seen as a natural act in the same way wild animals hunt each other. What is absolutely not okay is when an animal who is not wild, but supposedly civilized, as human beings consider themselves, directly abuses another animal or pays another person to commit the abuse. This completely goes against the natural order of predator and prey in the wild. We are treating animals like a product or a commodity to be used and discarded.

Like any movement against cruelty and abuse, being vegan is about the benefit to the victims, in this case animals. It is not about the potential benefit to the abusers in refraining from victimizing those being oppressed.

Dairy cows, for example, are forcibly impregnated by human beings with semen syringes. They also have their udders burned with an actual flamethrower as a means of killing germs. Yes, you read that right, *flamethrowers*. As if that wasn't bad enough, when a cow gives birth, her baby is immediately taken away to be isolated in a cage and plumped up to be sold as "veal." These babies are slaughtered at three to five weeks old. Even worse, male chicks in the egg industry are thrown into a meat grinder and macerated alive, mere hours after they hatch. This happens because it costs the animal abusers more money to raise them than it does to murder them at birth. This is quite obviously a shameful and monstrous practice that would *never* be tolerated for a dog or a cat.

Who can help them? We can. And we do this by refusing to buy the products the factory farming industry turns these animals into.

Our culture desensitizes people to the obscene cruelty and violence perpetrated against animals on a daily basis, for a profit. Even worse, some people have been tricked into believing a pig is less deserving of life than a dog. This delusion has reached such an extreme degree that people will feel literally no remorse eating bacon yet cry in anguish upon seeing a dog being beaten. This is emotional brainwashing at its finest. When you teach a child it's okay to kill and eat a pig but not a dog, you are teaching that child to discriminate. This culturally learned discrimination affects the way we look not only at animals, but at other humans who are different from us, thus feeding the culture of discrimination.

"To get mud off your hands, use soap and water. To get blood off your hands, go vegan."

—JOHN SAKARS

HEALTH AND ENVIRONMENTAL CONCERNS ABOUT EATING ANIMALS

Red meat is classified as a level two cancerous carcinogen. Why is this not front-page news? Why don't McDonald's and Burger King have to print that on their takeout containers the same way cigarette companies do? Not only does eating meat give us cancer, but breeding billions of animals into existence causes more yearly pollution than all forms of transportation combined. It's crazy to think this staggering statistic is true. This pollution wreaks havoc on ecosystems all around the planet, which makes it harder to grow things that actually promote good health like fruits and vegetables. Not only that, but people who live in the communities where these factory farms exist experience a host of different health issues due to breathing in the heavily polluted and toxic air.

In the groundbreaking documentary *Need to Grow*, conservationist Van Dana Shiva says, "We are creating a food scarcity system in the name of providing food!" That sentence woke up me up when I heard it. She is basically making the point that we are plundering mother nature and in the process undermining the very method through which we produce *real* food. We have plenty of food to feed starving populations, but our food prioritization and resource management is so poor we end up with millions of tons of food waste while millions of people go hungry. On top of that, the amount of grain we feed to livestock animals each year could literally end world hunger if distributed properly.

My primary reason for opposing this industry is, as I said before, to save the animals who are being taken advantage of in extremely cruel ways. But considering the ecological destruction this industry causes, it is a moral imperative that we stop supporting these practices. Everyone wants to see a better and more peaceful world, but many do not realize it starts with us as consumers refusing to pay for things that cause massive amounts of cruelty, destruction, and pollution.

People fall victim to an imagined state of affairs fabricated by cultural frameworks. Culture is the abstraction we buy into by identifying as law-abiding citizens rather than advanced animals who abide by the laws of nature. Instead of behaving like organisms in an environment, we behave like consumers in a marketplace. We worry about our lawns, our credit scores, and our favorite sports teams instead of our fitness, our health, our environment, and our fellow beings.

The evidence is conclusive: our diets are killing us. Not only that, but the five hundred million animals we slaughter every single day is ruining ecosystems and killing other life forms across the planet. I will never understand how someone is labeled as an extremist or radical for caring about that huge issue and refusing to participate. People who rescue abused cows and pigs are labeled as extremists and are criminally penalized. Meanwhile, people who rescue abused dogs are called heroes, and we make feel-good TV shows about them. It's not hard to see how foolish and naïve this behavior is.

It's just looked at as normal status quo behavior to keep on doing it. "Veganism" is regarded as one thing you could be passionate about or one thing you could be concerned about in the larger scheme of all the issues people care about. However, it's quite obvious it's the most important issue there could possibly be because the health of our planet is integral to our way of life.

"We are so much the victims of abstraction, that with the Earth in flames we can barely rouse ourselves to wander across the room and look at the thermostat."

—TERENCE MCKENNA

In modern society, we have been empowered to have immense control over our food choices—a luxury our ancestors did not have. The most fundamental and basic way we advance as organisms is by turning food into energy, and in turn using that energy to become ourselves. Our bodies recycle every cell within a period of seven years, and the only material we have to make new cells comes from the nutrients we take in. We have advanced as a species by learning the best ways to take care of our bodies, so to disregard our health undermines all the knowledge humanity has gained throughout so many generations of struggle.

If we are going to attempt to nourish ourselves with food that is known to be our bodies, while the production of this food creates toxicity in our environment, then we might as well not eat at all!

We have also advanced as a society by extending our definitions of inclusion and compassion to all individuals, not just those who are like us. Animals are no exception to these inclusions. We are simply one species of animal on this planet. We must stand together and put a stop to immoral acts against our fellow beings, rather than paying others to continue to do it while we turn a blind eye. This is the message!

"The problem is that humans have victimized animals to such a degree that they are not even considered victims. They are not even considered at all. They are nothing; they don't count; they don't matter. They are commodities like TV sets and cell phones. We have actually turned animals into inanimate objects—sandwiches and shoes."

—GARY YOUROFSKY

HOW CAN WE SAVE OUR PLANET?

In addition to the moral obligation any decent person feels to not torture animals, there is also an environmental obligation. Science has now proven and stated unequivocally that the single most effective change a person can make in reducing their carbon footprint is to stop consuming animal products. There it is. We know what we must do. It is not reasonable to ask people not to drive cars or consume water and other natural resources for our physiological and material needs. However, it is completely within reason to ask people not to consume animal products when we know how costly they are to the planet and to our health, animal suffering aside.

We are all part of one planetary environment. We all drink the same water, eat the same nutrients, and breathe the same air. Additionally, we all feel the same pain, the same hurt, the same loss, the same regret. Everything is connected. When we realize everything is one, we realize the suffering of one being is also our suffering. Just as we each benefit from the contributions of a large tree producing oxygen, we all suffer when that tree is cut down. When a prominent artist or musician dies, we all mourn the loss of their valuable contributions to the world. Yet when millions of acres of rainforest are cut down each year to make way for animal agriculture, we hardly ever mourn the trees and the resources we are losing. We must make the conscious decision to connect the dots of our mutual suffering.

"A human being experiences himself, his thoughts and feelings as something separated from the rest, a kind of optical delusion of consciousness. This delusion is a kind of prison for us, restricting us to our personal desires and to affection for a few persons nearest to us. Our task must be to free ourselves from this prison by widening our circle of compassion to embrace all living creatures and the whole of nature in its beauty."

—ALBERT EINSTEIN

A study of various populations on earth identified several areas known as the "blue zones." These are places with the highest percentage of people who regularly live to age one hundred or older. These areas also see much less frequent occurrence of dietary-influenced disease. The diets of these various groups of people were found to be comprised primarily of a food group known as pulses, which include legumes, beans, and lentils. Not only are pulses extremely good for our bodies, they're also good for the planet, with a very low carbon footprint and significantly less water usage than other foods. For example, it takes about forty-three gallons of water to produce one pound of pulses. But a farmer will use eight hundred to one thousand gallons of water to raise one pound of meat. It is not hard to see why our consumption of animals is an enormous problem.

"Conservation is the application of common sense to the common problems for the common good."

-—GIFFORD PINCHOT

As we all know, in late 2019, a strain of animal-borne coronavirus, COVID-19, mutated to deadly effect. The same exact thing happened in the early 2000s when the avian flu and swine flu—which came from a chicken farm and a pig farm, respectively—killed thousands of people in two deadly outbreaks. The most effective thing we can do to prevent this from happening again is to reduce our animal farming and eliminate factory farms altogether. The close quarters and unclean conditions present on factory farms are a breeding ground for bacteria and viruses just like COVID-19. We are lucky the COVID-19 strain was not more deadly than it is. There is no guarantee this will not happen again, and if we keep farming animals in these conditions, we are liable to cause a far deadlier viral outbreak. We must focus on conservation and use common sense to enact sensible policy change to prevent things like this from happening in the future.

Again, my reason for being vegan is primarily compassion for animals. Ever since that moment with the mother deer, I knew what I was participating in toward the animals was wrong. We don't show our children what happens in slaughterhouses because we don't want to traumatize them. Yet, we still feed them the products that come out of these death factories. We have to start admitting to ourselves that what we are doing to animals is wrong, because there's not going to be any moving forward until people start accepting that. It begins with our dollars and the conscious intent behind what they purchase. We must refuse to participate in that which is inhumane. It's about taking a stand and refusing to support an industry that's destroying the planet while its main business is exploiting animals. This must stop because we are more compassionate than that.

Some people do not see that it is wrong, and it is up to us as people who do see it to keep shining the light of compassion and awareness on the subject. This is the only way to liberate these animals from the massive suffering induced by our purchasing behaviors. In doing so, our health and the health of our planet will also flourish. It's as simple as the way we spend time. We try not to spend our time foolishly in ways that directly undermine our physical and environmental health and security. So, why are we spending our money in a way that we wouldn't spend our time?

People can even go vegan now and still go back to eating meat if they want because lab-grown meat made from stem cells is available in stores. If you're buying meat from farms, you're supporting animal abuse in the exact same way as if you were physically abusing the animal yourself, because you're paying for it to happen. Unfortunately, this is an unavoidable fact because even on farms where the animal is raised humanely, it is still subject to a life of captivity in a wasteful industry with an extremely laborious and low-yield production process compared to other, healthier protein alternatives. And of course, humane slaughter is an oxymoron. There is nothing humane about killing a being that does not want to die and does not need to die.

If all someone needs to do is take a vitamin B12 supplement to prevent animal suffering, that person is courageous for adopting that lifestyle and living out their values. It's not even like it's some crazy act, it's as simple as abstaining from eating the flesh of a living being if you can survive just fine without it and you wouldn't do this to the animal yourself. I fully expect the entire world to have woken up to this realization in fifty to one hundred years, but I don't expect everyone around me to behave exactly the way I do. All I can do is compassionately speak this message of truth and stand up for what I believe in. With every person who hears the message and changes their mind, the lives of countless animals are saved. It's up to you as an individual to bring about this change.

Individual decision is the driving force of social change.

I wrote this song as a cry for help. Our fellow beings are in peril, and their fates rest in the hands of each one of us. We can either act in a way consistent with our moral values and convictions, or we can turn a blind eye to the suffering and injustice our choices and purchasing behaviors are causing. I choose not to pay for animals to be abused. I choose not to pay for our natural resources to be plundered. I choose compassion, mindfulness, and responsible consumption.

How many more times will we allow these heinous acts to continue? If you still see nothing wrong with this situation, or you do see something wrong but are unwilling to change your behavior to address it, ask yourself one question:

Will you hold the knife?

"Everyone has to find what is right for them, and it is different for everyone. Eating, for me, is how you proclaim your beliefs three times a day... Three times a day, I remind myself that I value life and do not want to cause pain to or kill other living beings. That is why I eat the way I do."

—NATALIE PORTMAN

FATHERS AND SONS

———

It takes emotional skills to stay up and pay the bills
while your children are out goin' after their thrills
it just might kill you to think that
they're not comin' back

How do you do it, walkin' around this house
with no purpose to save you now
you can't, speak loud,
so you, seek out,
another way to say to me I love you
always questioning and wonderin', what's tomorrow
gonna bring?
my only choice is to sing, my only choice is to sing-

Have you ever seen the love between a father and son?
Have you ever dreamed of bein' somebody's number one?
Save yourself some time to be the person you never did
take away your pride and get in touch with that little kid

I don't need to wake up with the sunrise to be free
nothin' really matters but this moment , don't you see?

you don't have to wake up with the sunrise to be free
nothin' really matters but this moment, don't you see?

So take the chances you get, 'cuz the feelin' of regret
is a lesson you still haven't learned just yet
and it might disturb you to hear that
there's no goin' back

Be who you want to, never apologize,
for the sparkle that's in your eyes
you gotta' take flight, shine bright

Have you ever seen the love between a father and son?
Have you ever dreamed of bein' somebody's number one?
Save yourself some time to be the person you never did
Take away your pride and get in touch with that little kid,
inside

"The parent raises the child, and then the child raises the parent."

—UNKNOWN

I will never forget the look in my mother's eyes when she said to me, "Dad had a stroke." They were the most unsettling words I had ever heard. I can still remember the uneasiness I felt hearing her swift footsteps approaching the basement door before she called me upstairs. I had an eerie sense that something wasn't right. "Hold, on guys, something's wrong," I said to my bandmates. We were in the middle of practicing a new song, arguing a bit over who should play what part. Suddenly, none of that mattered.

All I could think about was whether my dad would be okay. An enormous wave of anxiety rushed over me as I contemplated the possibility that I might never get to see him or talk to him again. I asked myself, *Is this it? Do I have to be the man of the house now? Is it suddenly my responsibility to take care of my mom and my little brother? To take care of our house? How about his amazing garden—would all the plants die?* I didn't know how I would get through this day, let alone the rest of my life without him. There was still so much I had to learn, and I had never been more conscious of it than in that moment.

Luckily, my dad worked at a Navy base, and we received news from his coworkers that his condition had stabilized, and he was in good spirits at the hospital. However, we still had to wait several hours before we could go see him, so after the most terrifying forty-five minutes of my life, band practice resumed.

It was July 12, 2017. I was still living at home at the time, so I was playing my dad's drum set. My bandmates, Sam and Brendan, gave me a big hug to help me feel better. We were all shaken from the incident. My father has been a mentor to all three of us, not just in music, but in life. When I picked up his sticks again, I had a newfound appreciation for the beautiful vintage Rogers drum set before me. Not only that, but I think I played better than I ever had. There was so much raw emotion in my playing, so much gratitude I was channeling from deep within my heart. It was a profoundly transformative learning experience.

In the following days, I found myself thinking a lot more about how I spend my time. Something my dad always told me is that in life, when you don't give it your all, you're only cheating yourself. I didn't want to cheat myself anymore. In the wake of his stroke, I thought about all the ways I could do better in my life, all the opportunities I had let pass me by due to my own laziness and the privilege of not having to work nearly as hard as he did to get by.

I decided it was time to start living my life in a more intentional way. This meant spending more time with my family and friends and being grateful for the simple joys in life. It also meant embracing my creativity and committing fully to my career as a professional musician. Luckily, that resulted in my dad and I getting to jam together more—a lot more. Over the past few years, we've developed a great number of riffs we've turned into songs, combining our lyrical ideas and musical skills.

One day while planting tomatoes together, my dad referred to the soil he had chosen as "supercharged dirt." "It's got extra nutrients and properties that help the plants grow more easily," he said.

I was paying attention, but I couldn't stop thinking about what a great band name that would be. So that's what our project is called. *Supercharged Dirt*, pure rock and roll that hits unapologetically hard with a message of truth and empowerment.

I'm grateful to have the father I have. Being his son has taught me many lessons, but perhaps the most important one is the value of play. When a parent raises a child, a great deal of emphasis is placed on playtime, a goal-less exercise in exploring the world together. But as children get older, their parents don't play with them nearly as much. Children learn to play on their own as a way of developing a personality and a unique approach to problems, tasks, and challenges. This reduction in time spent playing together often causes parents and children to become emotionally disconnected from each other in adolescence and adulthood.

In addition, the parents, who grew up playing all the time as kids, and then subsequently played with their own kids, are suddenly not playing anymore. And people wonder why they aren't happy later in life! We absolutely need creative playtime if we want to be truly happy. Those of us who embrace this fundamental aspect of our existence continually cultivate a state of curiosity and open-mindedness about the world. This works wonders for our relationship with both ourselves and others.

Since my dad and I started playing music together, not only has our relationship improved, but we have developed a sixth sense musically, one which allows us to telepathically anticipate what the other person going to play, and when. We can start and stop on a dime, effortlessly, without planning it. This connection has strengthened our intuitive ability to know what the other is feeling and thinking when we are not playing music. Playing an instrument has been proven to be the single most beneficial activity for improving brain function and creative intelligence, but I would argue creative play in general is the single most important factor in our overall happiness in life. We can all benefit greatly from spending more time playing.

PUT THIS BOOK DOWN AND GO PLAY!

When was the last time you allowed your desires to dictate how you spent your time? Whether it be a day, a week, or even just one hour, following our natural curiosity can bring immense amounts of joy, and that joy can alleviate a lot of our suffering. Parents are often so busy taking care of their children, they forget about or neglect their own needs. Most people eventually realize they need to get more sleep, or they should be eating healthier and exercising more. But what many of us often forget is that play is just as essential to our overall health as any other activity. We are naturally inquisitive creatures, and denying ourselves the opportunity to explore our sense of wonder in a free and unstructured way can have a seriously negative impact on how we feel.

Life is not meant to be lived paycheck to paycheck, one forty- to fifty-hour workweek at a time. We say "TGIF—Thank God it's Friday!" Really? When someone says that, what I hear is, "Thank God 75 percent of my week is over and now I have the remaining 25 percent to forget about how much it sucks." If we made it a point to engage ourselves in a creative activity at least once a day, there would be no need to say TGIF. Instead, we can say "TGIP—Thank God I'm playing!"

REIGNITING YOUR INNER CREATIVE SPARK

What did you enjoy doing when you were a child? How did you feel while doing those activities? As a rule, children naturally do what appeals to them. Without societal and social pressures, judgments, and responsibilities, children follow the path to whatever delights them. They don't spend time worrying about the future when there are some really cool colorful toys to play with right in front of them. What are the cool, colorful toys in your life? Put down this book and go play with something!

Exercises to Try:

1. Draw a picture using your favorite colors. It can be abstract or a specific subject, whatever suits your current mood.

2. Research a topic you've been curious about for a while but haven't investigated. You never know what you'll discover!

3. Make a vision board by cutting out words and images from magazines that inspire you to feel abundant and depict your ideal future. :)

"If I had my child to raise all over again, I'd build self-esteem first, and the house later. I'd finger-paint more, and point the finger less. I would do less correcting and more connecting. I'd take my eyes off my watch, and watch with my eyes. I'd take more hikes and fly more kites. I'd stop playing serious, and seriously play. I would run through more fields and gaze at more stars. I'd do more hugging and less tugging."

—DIANE LOOMANS

TAKE ANOTHER DIME

———

I don't need to take another dime
This company is wastin' me and my time

It's time to wake up on my own
Time to forget the things I've known
Time to let go of places I have outgrown

I don't need to make it all worthwhile
All that matters now to me is my smile

It's time to set out on my own
Time to forget the things I've known
Time to let go of faces I have outgrown

Slow and steady, wins the race
Slow and steady, enjoys the pace
There's nothin' you can find
that ain't already inside your mind

You don't need to take another dime

"There is no passion to be found in playing small—in settling for a life that is less than the one you are capable of living."
—NELSON MANDELA

I'll never forget the day I arrived in Cuzco, Peru. Known as the spiritual epicenter of the world. Cuzco is a city located high in the Andes Mountain range, isolated from any surrounding towns. It is a necessary stop on the journey to Machu Picchu, the ancient mountaintop temple at the western edge of the Amazon jungle. How did I get here? And why does this chapter start off in Peru? It all stems back to a conversation I had with one of my best friends, Alex Sotis.

Alex and I met in college, and we became increasingly close over the following years, bonding over our mutual love of music, traveling, and the philosophy of the legendary Alan Watts. Alex had received his degree in mathematics and computer science and supported himself after college by making and selling beautiful copper and gemstone jewelry. Shortly thereafter, he accepted a programming job with a well-known software firm. After working there for a year, things were going well, and he was finding fulfillment in the challenges of his work, but something was missing. In our conversations, he would say things to me like "I just don't want to wake up in twenty years still working this job and living in Rhode Island." The wintertime was especially tough, and I recall him saying, "It sucks, man. I wake up, it's dark. I go into the office for eight hours, and when I come out, it's dark again. I feel like I don't have time to enjoy my life the way I want to."

I knew his pain all too well. I had been selling insurance and working odd jobs to support myself when I was just starting to play music professionally. I knew how soul-sucking the corporate world could be, especially in the winter when you are "spending all the sunlight hours of the day stuck inside a fluorescent-lit cubicle breathing recycled air," as Alex put it. I'll never forget that conversation.

We were standing on the roof of his apartment building, looking out over downtown Providence.

"The money is great," he said, "and I don't mind the job. If I could work from home, wake up, do yoga, go for walks, and avoid the commute, I feel like I'd be much happier." Something had to change for my friend, and soon.

In June of 2018, I invited Alex to attend a mindfulness retreat for young adults at Blue Cliff Monastery in New York.

"Hell yeah," he said. In addition to me and Alex, our friends Sam, Ryan, Tim, and Mark also decided to come. It was my first chance to experience this magical place with my best friends. What followed were five days of total bliss. In fact, Alex had such a healing, transformative, and overall life-changing experience that he decided to give up the lifestyle he knew altogether. The time at the monastery reoriented him to what truly mattered in life—his happiness. He was prepared to give up not just the comforts of his apartment, but also his salary, close relationships, and familiar environment to fulfill his dream of living in South America and learning to speak Spanish.

I remember feeling ecstatic when he told me, because this was a dream he'd been talking about for a while. I love it when people I love go for their dreams. Having visited Peru the previous summer, he decided that was a good place to start his journey.

"What's your plan?" I asked.

"I'm going to teach English," he replied, "and use my savings to find a cheap apartment with Wi-fi while I work on my Spanish. It only pays twenty dollars an hour, but the cost of living there is a third of what it is here in the states, so I'll be saving a ton of money."

"Wow," I said, admittedly feeling a bit jealous. "That sounds pretty nice!"

I was so proud of my friend, and so deeply grateful for the practice of mindfulness and the profound impact it can have on the lives of ordinary people. You don't need to be a monk or a spiritual guru to enjoy the benefits of what mindfulness has to offer. You simply have to trust the voice in your heart and give it time to rise above the noisy thoughts that constantly barrage the mind with chatter.

When you finally hear that voice and find the courage to pursue what makes you come alive, the universe will open doors for you where there were once roadblocks. When you make the commitment to yourself and your happiness, seemingly impossible things become easily attainable. Remember this, especially when you are afraid of making the leap toward your dreams!

Now here's the best part of the story...

A few months after the retreat, Alex decided to formally give his resignation at work. He gave his company five weeks' notice so they'd have time to prepare for his departure. But during that time, something extraordinary happened. The company decided to restructure the entire division in which Alex worked, resulting in him having a new boss. This new boss, upon hearing of Alex's intended resignation, called him in for a meeting.

In this meeting, he explained that Alex was a valued member of their team and asked if he'd be willing to stay with the company but just work remotely from South America. I was not there, but I can only imagine the feeling of disbelief on my friend's face upon hearing this news. This is what he had wanted all along. He actually enjoyed using his skills at work but wanted the freedom to enjoy his days outside of his stuffy, sunshine-deprived cubicle. Now he had the chance to do it, all while exploring a new country and saving even more money than if he'd taught English.

But wait—here's the kicker:

His new boss then asked him to name his salary!

Even more unbelievably, when Alex replied with a number that was a few dollars an hour more than what he was making, his boss suggested an even higher number—over ten dollars an hour higher than his original salary!

"We want to keep you interested," his boss said.

Alex was in disbelief and called me that day to tell me the news. I was quite shocked myself! I will never forget the sense of elation that filled me as we celebrated this incredible moment together.

THE RIPPLE EFFECT

Fast forward one year later, and there I was standing atop Machu Picchu, looking out over miles and miles of dense Amazonian rainforest. The energy at this ancient, sacred site is intensely palpable, and my consciousness was as relaxed as it had ever been in my life. While traveling through Peru, I had been reading a spiritual adventure novel called *The Celestine Prophecy* by James Redfield, which added to the excitement of the journey. Sitting inside of a section of Machu Picchu known as the Temple of the Condor, I wrote down the following entry in my journal:

My life purpose is becoming much clearer. I was born to my specific parents in order to synthesize their life views. To create stability through adventure. To discover happiness through play. And to serve others with my gifts. I know I am on the path. There may be occasional setbacks, but my resolve is strong. I flow easily in and out of all situations. I will be a beacon of light for myself primarily, but also for those around me, who, by becoming better, will in return enhance the quality of my own life, as I live in a world with more and more conscious people. Listening to my song "Safe as We Can" here atop Machu Picchu was an incredible experience. I am now realizing just how good my song is, all the intricacies, all the ways I dipped into the creative pool of the universe to achieve my ultimate vision. I'm about to get nominated for a GRAMMY!

It's happening to me for a reason. I'm not an imposter; I'm a hero at the beginning of his story. I have to believe that it is my truth, that I will continue to help heal people, that I will serve the highest good through whatever means necessary.

I will never forget writing this journal entry at Machu Picchu. I might not have had the opportunity to stay with Alex in Peru—which made my travel experience a lot easier—if I had not invited him to Blue Cliff. When we share value with other people, it pays back valuable dividends in our own lives.

ANOTHER DAY, ANOTHER DIME

Don't say to yourself, "I wish I could do what I love and still make money." Instead say, "How can I make money while still doing what I love?" Ask yourself that question and give your mind time to come up with an answer. Keep asking questions like this, and you will get new ideas. Eventually, you will find yourself acting on these ideas, and before you know it, you'll be earning money in ways you never thought possible.

Don't keep sacrificing your happiness today for the promise of happiness tomorrow.

The quality of your life depends on the quality of your days. When we decide to work jobs we hate instead of following our dreams, we are shortchanging ourselves. Remember that as you grow, you lift others around you, which comes back to you in the form of more positive energy in your environment.

You don't need a ton of money to be happy. Let it go and be open to the flow by following your desires and your intuitive guidance toward your dreams. If you do this, you will find exactly what you've been looking for!

"If you say that getting the money is the most important thing, you'll spend your life completely wasting your time. You'll be doing things you don't like doing in order to go on living, that is to go on doing things you don't like doing, which is stupid!"
—ALAN WATTS

TIP OF YOUR FINGER

———

In the tip of your finger,
All the magic in this world
And the thoughts we have that linger,
We can turn them into pearls

Walkin' outside my soul to see,
everybody stops to stare at me
I used to be afraid of bein' too loud,
but now I wear this smile, I wear it proud!

Everybody's got their own objective,
and everybody's got their own perspective
How can I take that Good Directive,
and make myself part of collective

Energy, can't you see, we're energy,
you and me, energy
In the tip of your finger

So how does it feel, when you open up your mind to somethin'
real?

How does it feel, when you realize there's so much you can heal?
With the tip of your finger

"The syntactical nature of reality, the real secret of magic, is that the world is made of words. And if you know the words that the world is made of, you can make of it whatever you wish."
—TERENCE MCKENNA

Let's step back in time to the day I wrote this song. It was a cold Sunday afternoon in autumn. I was preparing to fly to South America the next morning to visit my friend Alex, who was living in Peru at the time. While packing my suitcase, I was basking in the warm sunlight hitting my living room floor. I can vividly recall the way this radiant light was pouring in around the basil plant in my window, decorating my walls and ceiling with incredible shadows. It was a very peaceful, magical moment. At that same moment, my phone made a familiar noise. It was a voice message on WhatsApp from my friend Andreas in Germany. We regularly leave each other voice messages to share cool updates and details from our lives. That particular day, however, he shared an idea that inspired me to write this song.

Andreas had sat down on a bench in a beautiful park in Bonn, the city where Beethoven was born. He was watching a group of doves flying back and forth, going about their business. The birds were looking for crumbs of food and meandering around the cobblestones that surrounded the nearby fountain. He shared with me his sense of wonder and awe over the realization that these birds seemed so intelligent, so aware, and so adept at their natural instinctive behaviors, despite having a brain the size of the "tip of your pinky finger." His observations amused me, and I found myself inspired with an idea for a song.

When his words cut out, I heard a very magical melody bouncing around inside the walls of my brain. Tiny electrical impulses were causing me to hear a particular piece of music in my head as a direct result of his words. I grabbed my acoustic guitar, and the lyrics began to flow. The coolest part about writing this song was the awareness that I was actively channeling the very same magic I was referring to in the lyrics to compose the song! My fingers exerted the magic touch onto the guitar, which in turn produced the vibrations necessary to create a sound that captured my ecstatic feeling of being alive in the present moment. Within minutes, I had a recording on my phone and sent it to Andreas.

"Wow man, it's an instant hit!" he said back to me in a voice message. "I love it. I'm so glad my words inspired you in such a way."

We eventually ended up talking on the phone, and I shared some news about what I had been up to that weekend.

The night before, I had performed as the headlining act at an awards show for all the artists from New England that had made the official ballot for the 2020 GRAMMY Awards. It was an exciting event during which I received recognition for my artistic contributions to the community. I felt so validated by how many people came out to support me and the other artists. People were genuinely thankful to hear our music, and proud of the talent coming out of our little state.

I felt additionally proud of myself, too, because I hosted and served as the emcee and sound engineer for the event. I thought back to all the times I had been told I was too talkative in school by my teachers, all the times I had been silenced when trying to express myself. Well, now it was my turn to bask in the glory of the moment and celebrate the success my self-expression had created.

Somewhere along the line, I must have subconsciously adopted the belief that my teachers were right. I believed I really was too loud and disruptive. I used to worry all the time that I was talking too much or that people wouldn't care what I had to say. These thoughts served as self-limiting beliefs which prevented me from sharing all that my heart wanted to express. I knew it wasn't true, but I just couldn't get it out of my head. This belief caused me to have lingering doubts about the validity of my own point of view. I would like to offer a metaphor here for anyone who may find themselves plagued with these kinds of thoughts.

TURNING PAIN INTO PEARLS

Do you know the reason why oysters make pearls? If not, the answer may surprise you!

Oysters try to keep the inside of their shells clean and safe, like any creature would. When a piece of debris or otherwise unwanted object such as a grain of sand gets inside an oyster's shell, it can seriously irritate and disturb the organism. Unlike other creatures, oysters have an interesting way of dealing with a problem like this.

Since they have no limbs with which to physically remove the irritant from their shell, they have to get creative. They produce a mineral substance called nacre, a.k.a. mother of pearl, the same material their shells are made of. The nacre hardens around the outside of the piece of debris, coating it in several layers of this smooth material. The result of this process is a soft, shiny pearl that no longer causes the oyster irritation!

Fascinating, right? Now close your eyes for a moment and picture your mind as the inside of the oyster's shell. We cannot physically remove negative thoughts or feelings with our hands. But we can instead use our innate creative power to transform that which irritates us, and in the process soothe our pain.

As a musician, I experience this all the time. Back when I was first starting to play the guitar, I found it provided me an outlet to channel my emotions and shift my perspective. Even if I was feeling upset, the mere act of playing allowed my mind to wander and disengage from negative thoughts. In this way, I was able to take negative thoughts and reframe them in a positive light.

Maintaining a positive attitude is not always easy, but when I am down, or even just feeling off, playing music works just about every time to help me relax. I don't have to be playing intentionally or trying to create a song. The simple act of interacting with the instrument allows me to drop into the present moment and experience something new. Rather than being stuck in regret from the past or anxiety about the future, I am then fully present with myself and my environment.

Perhaps you have you tried this yourself and experienced the benefits. If you haven't, I encourage you to try exploring your creativity when you need a change of mental scenery. Even if it's something simple like doodling on a notebook page, or singing in the car, creative acts can help the mind move through negative feelings. The point is not to put pressure on yourself to create something perfect, or even good for that matter. Just simply finding joy in the creative act in and of itself can be highly therapeutic.

As I have spent time developing my songwriting skills, I've noticed how the process of writing lyrics has helped me change the way I see myself and my past experiences. In this particular song, I was able to reframe my self-doubt as self-confidence. And as an added benefit, the resulting pearls of wisdom have provided beauty and value not just to me, but also to the people I've played this song for at concerts and retreats.

MAKING MAGIC HAPPEN

It is truly incredible how much love we can bring into reality when we lean into the feeling of creative ecstasy that comes from self-expression. Our hands are powerful tools for constructing the world around us, but our thoughts and words are much, much more powerful. Music combines what our hands are doing with what our thoughts and words are doing for an extra potent dose of magic power!

You can give someone the best advice in the world, but there is no guarantee they will follow it. Most people don't like being told what to do. But give them that same advice in the form of a good song, and it's a completely different story. Why? Because music is the spoon full of sugar that helps the medicine go down. The sweet vibrations put us in a positive emotional state so we can be receptive to the message in the lyrics. That's where the magic lies!

When I say magic, I don't mean turning people into frogs or casting spells like a wizard. However, it is interesting to note that the word "spell" has multiple meanings. Most commonly, we use it as the definition for putting letters together to create words, which in turn create meaning. Another definition of spell, as in "to be put under a spell," means to become enchanted, or to enter a trance-like state.

To cast a spell means to exert power over ourselves and the external world. Music has this power. It effects not only our minds, but our bodies, too. And because of this, music is the most powerful form of influence we have.

The official Merriam-Webster definition of a spell in this context is "a spoken word or form of words held to have magic power," or "a strong compelling influence or attraction." In my opinion, it is no coincidence that spelling and casting spells share these seemingly dissimilar definitions. When we look more deeply, we begin to notice how our words and speech affect not only the way we feel, but the way others are feeling too. We can turn someone's entire day around with a kind word. We possess that power within us!

However, we can also cause someone to feel absolutely worthless with our words. If we want to live mindfully, we must cultivate an awareness of how our words are impacting ourselves and those around us. We must make the effort to improve the quality of our speech and our comments. In this way, our reality will also improve.

You may have heard the expression, "With great power comes great responsibility." This adage has always resonated with me, perhaps because it is so simple. The more influence you have over a situation, the more responsible you are for the outcomes of that situation.

When we are being mindful artists, we can bring healing into the lives of many people. But first, we must acknowledge the power we possess. Only then can we assume the responsibility of creating a better world for ourselves and those around us. The energy of mindfulness, when applied to music, can transform a broken heart into a soul that sings!

"Creativity can solve almost any problem. The creative act, the defeat of habit by originality, overcomes everything."
—GEORGE LOIS

WRITE THIS DOWN

———

I don't need to write this down, It lives inside of me
I don't need to write this down, It lives inside of me, yeah

We don't need to write this down, It lives inside of us,
We don't need to write this down, It lives inside of us,
Get on the bus...

Cuz I'm a teacher, I'm a preacher,
just singin' my songs
hopin' everybody will sing along
I will meet ya, I will greet ya,
somewhere in between
reality and my sacred dream

But ya gotta be strong, ya gotta be wise,
Ya gotta be willin' to compromise
Ya gotta be bold, ya gotta be kind
gotta be the one thing you can't find
We gotta have faith, we gotta stand tall,
gotta believe we can move that wall
inside of us...just get on the bus

We don't need to write this down, It lives inside of us,
We don't need to write this down, It lives inside of us,
Get on the bus...

Cuz we're all teachers, we're all preachers,
just singin' our songs
hopin' everybody will sing along
We will meet ya, We will greet ya,
somewhere in between
reality and our sacred dreams

But we gotta be strong, we gotta be wise,
we gotta be willin to compromise
We gotta be bold, we gotta be kind
gotta be the one thing we can't find
We gotta have faith, we gotta stand tall,
gotta believe we can move that wall
inside of us...just get on the bus

We don't need to write this down, It lives inside of us
We don't need to write this down, It lives inside of us, yeah

"You didn't come into this world. You came out of it, like a wave
from the ocean. You are not a stranger here. You don't need to
do anything, because if you see yourself in the correct way, you
are all as much extraordinary phenomenon of nature as trees,
clouds, the patterns in running water, the flickering of fire, the
arrangement of the stars, and the form of a galaxy. You are
all just like that, and there is nothing wrong with you at all."

—ALAN WATTS

"*Dammit!*" I exclaimed. After driving over one hundred miles away from Asheville en route to Memphis, I realized I had left an important bag behind at my friend Kevin's house. It contained not only my travel fanny-pack, but also a package of relaxing herbs I was hoping to use on our long drive.

I was annoyed at myself and questioned whether it was worth going back for the items. Being the great friend he is, Andreas reassured me it was no big deal. He set my mind to ease and remarked, "We'll just get to our hotel at 11 p.m. instead of 8 p.m. No worries, my brother!"

He began turning around to take us back and retrieve the items. At the time, we had no idea what a glorious surprise awaited us back in Asheville.

When we arrived, Kevin led me to where I had left my bag. I felt relieved and decided to share one of the lavender and mullein infused herbal smokes with him. We chatted for a few minutes, and I was about to say goodbye again, when he stopped me.

"Hey man," he said, "I totally forgot to ask you before you left last time. I have a few of these mushroom chocolates left that my friend made. Do you guys want any?"

"Absolutely!" I exclaimed.

I was overjoyed! Andreas and I decided one would be enough, and that we would split it on our day off the next week.

The moment came that following Tuesday, after we left New Orleans. Despite the weather being below thirty degrees for our entire trip, this particular day happened to be about sixty degrees—a pleasant surprise for both of us. I searched on the map and located an incredible nature park just outside of Mobile, Alabama called Muddy Creek Trail. We decided to spend the day outside and eat the chocolate there. It is an absolutely idyllic place, featuring huge evergreen trees dotted almost uniformly over several acres.

The tree trunks were trimmed so there were no branches below five or six feet. Because of that, it was possible to see through the forest for a hundred feet or so before it faded to black. The beautifully eerie forest was balanced out by a large, enchanting meadow adjacent to it. We sat down in the meadow and Andreas took out his notebook and began writing as a way of expressing the beautiful thoughts and feelings beginning to wash over him. I got up and found a nice shady tree under which to play my guitar.

By that time, my altered state of consciousness had kicked in. I felt so happy, so peaceful, and so connected to the landscape around me. The park was indeed enchanting, and I was in just the right state of mind to appreciate it on a much deeper level than is normally possible. I noticed an awareness rising within me that I was not separate from this place. I remember thinking:

I am an animal, and this is my environment.
We are energetically tied together, as my

breath feeds the trees, and they feed me. But on top of that, I am a divine being. I have the power to access dimensions of reality normally hidden from conscious awareness.

I remember feeling so much love and connection in that moment, enjoying my journey peacefully under the shady tree. There was a sense of magic in the air. I was contemplating how I could share this vision with others, specifically my family. I wanted my parents to know why I do what I do, why I have dedicated my life to music. The incredible power I feel when playing music is difficult to convey at times. It's not a power based on dominance, but rather, enchantment. I began speaking aloud as if I was talking to an audience. In a way, it felt like the trees were listening to me.

I talked about how weird it feels sometimes to be a professional musician, having people refer to you as a rock star, and assuming your life is easy or perfect. Society glamorizes the lives of celebrities and rock stars as some glorious position to be attained. People idolize professional musicians to the degree of discounting their own worth compared to this person of celebrity status.

What is that personality representing for those people? What is that personality able to do for those people? What is it they feel they are getting from these people that they can't give to themselves? I was asking myself, as a professional musician, what is my real role here? What am I supposed to be providing for people that they can't just provide for themselves?

And it feels so weird because it's like, wait a second, hold on... I'm now living inside of this thing that, for other people, is supposed to represent ultimate glory or ultimate success. Yet here I am, just living my life, putting my shoes on one foot at a time just like the average person. I'm just a guy who loves rock and roll so much I decided to play it!

What am I doing that the average person cannot also do? What's on the other side of this imaginary line people are drawing in the sand? I was realizing how people are continually looking for something outside of themselves, and that's when it hit me. What everybody is searching for lives right inside of you! Right in the one place where you're not looking!

You <u>are</u> the path.

Upon having this realization, the lyrics began to flow. It felt like the whole forest was now tuned in to what I was saying and playing. I could feel the trees giving me their energy and attention, watching my every move. They were encouraging me to go on, to keep playing in order to discover more aspects of this hidden truth.

Happiness does not have to depend on the conditions outside of us. The music is already within us. We are the vehicle through which it takes form.

Music is a tool for discovering new aspects of reality and of ourselves. When combined with a consciousness-enhancing teacher like the psilocybin mushroom, the vibrations of music take us on a journey much deeper than what is normally possible.

In the midst of creating this song, I was having the most complex and mystical thoughts. I remember thinking about my parents and my brother, about how I wished I could communicate to them what it is I am really doing with music. A song is the result of bringing your heart out into the open, and I was yearning for connection with other people who understood the profound truths I was experiencing.

After playing the guitar part for a few more minutes, I came up with the lyric about hoping everybody would sing along. I sang it a few times to myself, wishing I had some backup vocals.

That's when I noticed two men walking along the path back to the parking lot. I smiled at them, and they smiled and nodded back. Something came over me in that moment, and I decided to stand up and walk over to them.

"Hey, will you guys sing with me?" I asked.

These two southern gentlemen were very surprised to hear my question.

"I'm a professional musician, on tour from Rhode Island," I said. "I'm working on this song, and I was wondering if you guys would sing along with me?"

"Well...we don't sing, but we'll listen to ya!" the older gentleman said in a thick, southern accent.

David and Jason were an uncle and nephew who work together and were out for a walk after finishing their job for the day. They listened to my song and said they really liked it! We then had a conversation about the music industry and what it's like traveling and playing shows. They were very interested in what I had to say. At their request, I played some of my original songs and a few cover songs.

Eventually, Andreas noticed me standing up talking to strangers—something not so common when you're in the middle of a psychedelic journey—and walked over to join us. We continued talking about what it's like to be on the road as a musician, meeting new people just like this. I shared with them how I had been reflecting on the fact that I'm just like the average person, except I happen to play music professionally.

Being the amazing friend he is, Andreas interjected:

"He's not just a professional musician, he's a *GRAMMY ballot artist!*"

Both David and Jason's jaws dropped at this new information. David was flabbergasted and asked if they could get a picture with us. I blushed, especially considering the nature of my reflections about celebrity under the tree, but I happily obliged, realizing my presence was serving as a source of inspiration for these new friends of ours. I started to lean into the feeling of connection I had cultivated before getting up from the tree.

Before they left, David asked us to play a song. Earlier in the week, Andreas and I had been singing "The Sound of Silence" by Simon and Garfunkel. We sang a duet of the song, and despite our guitars being noticeably out of tune with each other, it somehow sounded amazing! The men gave us a round of applause as the song finished and we took a playful bow.

"Well, we really didn't expect this on a Tuesday afternoon!" David said as he and Jason started to head back to their truck.

"Keep rockin' guys, and don't forget about us when you're famous!"

THE POWER OF GOING WITH THE FLOW

Have you ever beat yourself up about something you did, perhaps a mistake you made, only to later realize it actually led to something amazing? I know I certainly have, and it's easy to get down on yourself when things aren't looking good in the moment. As human beings, we can be so short-sighted sometimes. The funny thing is this song would not exist if I hadn't made an epic blunder leaving Asheville.

Now I'm going to share one of my favorite stories of all time. The following is an ancient Chinese parable dated back to over two thousand years ago. I'm confident you will see the wisdom present here in the parable of the Chinese farmer. It goes like this:

There once was a poor farmer who worked the soil with his son and their horse, and one day their horse ran away. The farmer's neighbor came over and said, "This is terrible! What an awful thing!"

The farmer replied, "Maybe so…and maybe not."

Two days later, the horse returned, but not alone. It brought a second horse with it. The neighbor said, "This is wonderful! What great luck!" Again, the farmer replied, "Maybe so… and maybe not."

A few weeks later, the farmer's son fell off the new horse and badly broke his leg. The neighbor again stopped by to say, "How horrible! Surely you have been cursed." Again, the farmer replied, "Maybe so… and maybe not."

Shortly thereafter, all the young men in the village were drafted to go and help fight off an invading army. Many of them died, but the farmer's son was spared from the draft because of his broken leg. The neighbor told the farmer how lucky he was.

And yet again, the farmer replied, "Maybe so… and maybe not."

What this story teaches us is obvious, but the moments at which it is applicable in everyday life are often not so obvious. It is truly difficult to remain mindful enough to not judge a particular event as good or bad until we have learned more information. We tend to categorize everything we experience as a way of organizing and making sense of life. Often, we don't wait long enough to see how an event will unfold over time, and what new possibilities it will create. Sometimes, an event we thought was the end of our life turns out to be a new beginning.

If I had not forgotten my bag in Asheville that day, this song would not exist. I have since played this song at concerts and plant medicine ceremonies all around the country. People have told me how much it healed them and how grateful they are for my music. How confused would I have been if my future self had interrupted my aggravation that day and said, "Nate, you were meant to forget that bag. It's going to lead to healing for a lot of people"?

Of course, it's impossible to predict the future, which makes it easy to get down on ourselves in the moment. My disorganization and forgetfulness had always been framed by others as something lacking in my life, something I needed to work on. But in this case, it was the very source of a chain of events that led to the creation of this beautiful song. It would not have come to me if I had not forgotten that bag. In my frustration, I didn't even realize there was a song waiting to come out of the experience. And the best part is, it was already inside of me, just like the song says.

"The sun shines not on us but in us. The rivers flow not past, but through us. Thrilling, tingling, vibrating every fiber and cell of the substance of our bodies, making them glide and sing. The trees wave and the flowers bloom in our bodies as well as our souls, and every bird song, wind song, and tremendous

storm song of the rocks in the heart of the mountains is our
song, our very own, and sings our love."

—JOHN MUIR

ONE DAY

———

One day, is all that is takes
One day, see the difference it makes
One day, we'll forget our mistakes
One day

One day, it takes effort and time
One day, it's gonna be mine
One day, I'll find another rhyme
One day

See the line in the sand that I drew with my hand
cuz I wanna understand but I don't have a plan
Runnin' outta' time way too much on my mind

If I knew what to do I'd share it with all of you
But I don't have a clue
and I'm still learnin' too

But if somethin' should break my stride
If I had nowhere to hide
I wonder if I could make it better

If someone would show me how
Then I'd be alright for now
I believe that I could make it better, one day...
One day at a time

See the line in the sand that I drew with my hand
cuz I wanna understand but I don't have a plan
Runnin' outta' time way too much on my mind

If I knew what to do I'd share it with all of you
But I don't have a clue
and I'm still learnin' too...

But if somethin' should break my stride
If I had nowhere to hide
I wonder if I could make it better
If someone would show me how
Then I'd be alright for now
I believe that I can make it better, one day...
One day at a time

One day, is all that is takes
One day, see the difference it makes
One day, we'll forget our mistakes
One day...

One day, it takes effort and time
One day, it's gonna be mine
One day, this heart's gonna shine
One day...

"One moment can change a day, one day can change a life, and one life can change the world."

—GAUTAMA BUDDHA

Promptly after returning the rental car from my two-week tour down south with Andreas, an interesting synchronicity occurred. The rental car office happened to be less than a mile from my friend Ryan's apartment, and for some reason, my intuition was telling me to stop by and pay him a visit. I had no idea if he would be home or not since he is a tradesman and often works weekends. To my surprise, as I pulled into his apartment complex, I noticed not only Ryan, but his mom Rhonda, standing outside. They were unloading groceries into the house at that very moment. Seeing Rhonda took me by even more surprise because she lives 1,400 miles away in Florida. I began to ask myself why this synchronicity was occurring.

They were both surprised and happy to see me. After I helped them bring the groceries inside, I decided to stay and hang out for a little while. We started catching up, and I told them about my travels with Andreas and my recent GRAMMY Award contention. Rhonda was impressed and asked me some questions about my career.

"So, you want to do music full time and really go for it, right?" she asked. "You really love it, playing music for a living?"

Her eager questions filled me with a sense of inner validation. Indeed, I had demonstrated to myself and those around me the ability to be successful in pursuing my goals and turning my dreams into a reality. What sat at the back of my mind, however, was that it still felt inauthentic in some way I couldn't quite place. Realizing I was getting lost in thought, I responded back with a resounding, "Yes," a big smile, and a proud look in my eyes.

"I really do," I said. "I've realized I can make a difference doing something I love and positively impact the world at the same time by continuing to follow this path."

Rhonda knows a thing or two about making a difference in the world. She has been on the front lines of the mental health field as a social worker and substance abuse counselor for over thirty-five years! I knew she had a lot of wisdom to share. However, I could never have been prepared for what she said to me next:

"You know, Nate, in all my years of working in my field I've always wanted to make a difference. But a few years ago, when I was diagnosed with breast cancer, and I was in the hospital with a brain tumor, some days it was hard to even get out of bed and just be myself, let alone help others. If someone could get me out of bed even one day a month, when I used to stay in bed for two to three weeks straight—if just one day I could get up and walk around, that was enough to make a big difference. Sometimes all it takes is one day."

I was absolutely floored. We've all experienced our share of hardships in life, but I knew that my then-twenty-six-year-old self could not possibly comprehend the intensity or stress Rhonda had been through on a personal level. I realized trying to understand it or put myself in her shoes was futile, but

I also realized her story was a lesson. It finally made sense to me why this synchronicity had occurred, and why I felt the urge to visit Ryan. My intuition was pointing me in the direction of a positive growth experience, and all I had to do was listen. After reflecting on what Rhonda shared, I knew a song was just waiting to be written.

The words kept ringing in my head: "One day, is all that it takes."

The very next day, I hung out with my friend Nicole at her house. Nicole and I had met just two weeks earlier by way of a chance encounter at a local park. She was out for a walk with her dog, Simon. In truth, she wasn't walking; she was riding her longboard while Simon pulled her. I thought this was interesting and felt a hunch to talk to her, but they were moving pretty fast. Not five minutes later, we crossed paths yet again. I took this as a sign and stopped to say hello and pet Simon. I told her I had my longboard in my trunk, so she came over to check it out with me.

I have a street stick I use with my longboard, which actually enables me to push off the ground, like paddling a kayak on land. Nicole was intrigued by this and wanted to give it a try. I held Simon's leash while she had some fun. After that, we decided to walk together and discovered we both love music and play guitar, we both listen to the same podcasts, and we both have a deep interest in spirituality and metaphysics. I played some of my songs for her on my phone and she really liked them.

"I love the vibe of your music," she said. "It's chill but deep at the same time."

Her remark stuck with me and gave me some positive inspiration for the tour.

When I got back, were having a relaxing Sunday evening together, talking about life and different spiritual ideas. She knew I had just returned from my tour and was eager to hear some stories. I began catching her up on the amazing synchronicities I encountered. After telling her the story of how "Write This Down" came to be, she broke out her acoustic guitar and asked me to tune it up for her. We sang some songs together, and after we finished, I mentioned my conversation with Rhonda and Ryan the day before. I asked if she wanted to help me write a new song based around the idea of "one day." She said yes, and within minutes we had a solid foundation for a song.

After a few practice runs working out the melody, I recorded a draft version into the voice memos app on my phone. When we listened back, we couldn't believe how good it sounded! Since I typically write songs alone, it was wonderful to experience how fun the songwriting process can be with another person there to help guide the flow and provide an audience. The song had basically written itself in a matter of minutes!

However, when I listened again the next day, something felt off. I couldn't quite place the feeling I got while listening to it. I was unsure if the song needed something more or if I was just second-guessing my work because of how easily and naturally it had come together. It was a classic case of imposter syndrome starting to kick in.

Later that evening, my best friend and former bandmate Brendan came over to my house to catch up and hear about my tour. Brendan is a gifted songwriter in his own right, and his style is unmistakably unique and different, leaning toward alternative rock. When I played the demo recording of "One Day" for him, he was blown away. Even though the song has a very pop feel to it, the natural flow of the rhythm and truth of the lyrics won him over.

Noticing how genuine Brendan's positive reaction was, I was confident the song was just as good as it had seemed the day before. I knew it still needed work, but I decided not to force it. In typical "organic song" fashion, I trusted that the necessary parts would come to me when it was time. Until then, I was content to keep playing and singing it, confident that inspiration would strike at the right moment.

Later that same week, I was on vacation with my dad in Punta Cana, Dominican Republic. The morning after we arrived at our hotel, I began journaling out on the balcony of our room. The hotel was right on the beach, and a sense of idyllic calm washed over me as I stared out over the endless turquoise water. That particular day, I was so excited to have traded in the winter blues of New England for the paradise before me. I've always found something so relaxing and refreshing about tropical landscapes. From the warm breezes to the vibrant colors and incredible sunsets, something about the atmosphere of the Caribbean is deeply soothing to my soul.

I remember feeling like something awesome was going to happen that day, but I had no idea what I was in for!

When I walked down to the beach, I noticed a man sitting at a table creating handmade jewelry. He was wrapping beautiful gemstones in copper, silver, and other precious metals, the same way my friend Alex did. I introduced myself in Spanish and asked if I could sit down, but I received a puzzled look in return. As it turns out, the man spoke English and was from Massachusetts, less than an hour from where I live!

"Name's Matthew," he said, "but you can call me Matt. I like your stone!" He was referring to the copper-wrapped Tiger's Eye pendant I was wearing.

"Thanks!" I said. "My best friend made it for me. He wraps stones just like you."

Matt and I quickly became friends, and he asked what I do for a living. I told him I was a professional musician and artist.

"I'm working on an album of acoustic songs right now," I said.

"That's cool. What's your style?" he asked.

I never know what to say when someone asks this question. I always want to let my songs do the talking and see what people think.

"Mind if I play you a song or two off my phone?" I asked. "You can be the judge and tell me how the music strikes you."

"Sure," he said. "It'll be nice to have something to listen to while I wrap."

Throughout our conversation, Matt continued to focus on making his jewelry. However, when I played him the demo of "One Day," he had to put his tools down. Tears began to fill his eyes. When the song ended, he just sat there, looking out over the ocean, clearly in a state of reflection. It was obvious he liked it, so I decided to take a moment to reflect as well.

Matt broke the silence a minute or two later and was effusive with praise for my musical talent and songwriting abilities.

"I've been blessed to know many amazing musicians in my life, and you're right up there with them man," he said. "That was fantastic. Made me reflect on a lot of things in my life."

Compliments like these always make me feel great because I feel it's much more important for my music to be relatable and leave an impression than it is for me to be the best guitarist or singer. I thanked Matt for his kind words and was about to tell him the story behind the song when he spoke again.

"You know, your style reminds me of a childhood friend of mine who went on to become really successful with his music. You might know him; his name's Matt Nathanson."

I was blown away.

Not only had I just been compared to an internationally famous acoustic rock star, but I had been listening to his song "Come on Get Higher" on the plane ride down to Punta

Cana! Synchronicity had struck again, this time in the form of a chance encounter with a genuine new fan and friend. Thinking back to the moment when I decided to stop by Ryan's house the previous weekend, I found great joy in how the synchronicity had come full circle.

THE POWER OF ONE DAY

In all the moments I spent writing and working on the song, I maintained focus on the initial message Rhonda had given me. It really is true that one day can change your live forever. However, we must always remember every single day is that one day. We have the power to create meaningful change each day of our lives, and we never know who that change will affect! People tell me this song is one of my best, and I attribute that to the mindful reflection that went into its creation. When we look deeply into the real lives, experiences, and feelings of those around us, there is plenty of treasure to discover.

Remember, one day is all that it takes!

"Wholeheartedly do what it takes to awaken your clear-seeing intelligence, but one day at a time, one moment at a time. If we live that way, we will benefit this earth."

—PEMA CHODRON

COME FIND ME

Everybody seems to want ya to find somethin' you believe,
But I'm the kind of guy who wears his heart out on his sleeve
The magic of the universe is where the answers lie,
But don't expect to find me here just waitin' around...
just waitin' around, to die

I've been lookin' for an opening down into the sublime
I guess I'll have to wait my turn and see what I will find
The message is the music and the music is the way
That we can reach the masses and inspire ourselves to play

So come find me when it's time, I believe that you were meant
to be mine
Oh come find me when it's time, I believe that you were
meant to be mine

What if all the lonely people got together to be sad?
Imagine all the fun they'd almost wish they never had...
There's somethin' deeper hidden in the meaning of this song,
See if you can catch my drift and start to sing along

So come find me when it's time, I believe that you were meant
to be mine
Oh come find me when it's time, I believe that you
were meant...
you were meant to be mine, all mine, all mine...

Oh come find me when it's time,
I believe that you were meant...
you were meant to be mine

*"People think a soul mate is your perfect fit, and that's what
everyone wants. But a true soul mate is a mirror, the person
who shows you everything that is holding you back, the person who brings you to your own attention so you can change
your life."*

—ELIZABETH GILBERT

It all started on a Friday the thirteenth. This was no ordinary
Friday the thirteenth, however. The day began in almost as
crazy a way as it finished. I woke up in the morning and had
a slight headache. These can quickly turn into migraines for
me, and I was scheduled to play a show later that night. So,
after drinking plenty of water, I decided to take a micro-dose
of LSD. It was ever so slightly noticeable in the background of
my awareness. As I had hoped, my headache subsided, and I
went about my day as usual. I felt funky, happy, and peaceful.

Unaware at the time that it would be my last show for quite
a while due to the COVID-19 lockdowns, I was blissfully
singing away and taking requests from the patrons. What
happened next altered the course of my entire life. About

halfway through my show, a woman in the audience who had just arrived requested I play some of my original songs. She was enjoying my performance a lot, to the point she had turned around completely in her chair to watch me play.

"You must have some original songs, right?" she asked. I nodded my head and played my song "Can't Be Wrong," including the harmonica part. When I finished, she was enthusiastically clapping and cheering with delight.

"I love it!" she said. "Do you have any others?"

Upon her request, I played "Organic Song" and "Fly." After more effusive praise, I took a break to get some water and thanked her for her kind words.

"My name's Tara," she said with a warm, inviting smile. The next words she spoke caught me off guard, in the best way possible. Skipping the formalities, she got right down to business and asked me a very important question.

"How do you feel about psychedelics?" she asked, with a coy smile.

I was unsure how to respond in the moment, but according to her, the look in my eyes said everything. Considering I had micro-dosed LSD that very same morning, her question was quite poignant. Before I had even uttered a response, she spoke again.

"I had a feeling," she said while giggling.

I went on to tell her about my relationship with psilocybin mushrooms, and the profound growth and healing I'd experienced with their help. As it turned out, Tara was no stranger to this kind of experience. When I inquired as to what her relationship with psychedelics was, her answer got me very excited.

"I'm a psychiatric mental health nurse studying to get my practitioner's license," she said, "and it's my dream to one day prescribe MDMA, psilocybin, and other plant medicines to help people struggling with mental illnesses like depression, anxiety, and PTSD. The research is already so promising!"

"Wow," I said, "we are going to have a lot to talk about!"

I personally am an outspoken advocate for this type of therapy, as well as our sovereign right as human beings to explore our consciousness on our own terms. Naturally, I was intrigued to learn more about this incredible human I had just met who seemed to share my perspective.

We exchanged contact information and hung out several times over the next few weeks, getting to know each other while painting and practicing our acro-yoga skills with a few of her friends. On the very first night we hung out, an interesting synchronicity occurred just before I left. We were sitting inside the circle of a giant hula-hoop on the floor when Tara started to ask me a question. Before she could finish, I telepathically knew what she was going to say.

"Have you ever read the—"

"*The Celestine Prophecy*?" I replied.

"Holy sh... *How the?*" she exclaimed.

In that moment, we discovered we were both huge fans of this life changing book. Written by James Redfield, the story follows a man traveling around Peru looking for knowledge about a series of ancient scrolls. The scrolls are comprised of nine insights which are purported to contain lost wisdom that will help humanity grow and evolve. Ironically, one of the book's central themes is that if you feel intrigued when you meet someone, it's because they have an important message for you. At this point, there was no hiding that Tara and I had quite a bit in common, but we had just met and were still nothing more than friends. However, our relationship did take on a new form a few weeks later. Feeling inspired by my expression of my musical talent and skills, Tara decided she wanted to take music lessons from me!

She initially wanted drum lessons, but a few weeks later decided she wanted to learn the guitar too. I realized the depth of my knowledge and learned a lot through the process of explaining what I know about music to her through a psychedelic lens. We talked about the magic of musical creation and how the vibrations actually affect our biochemistry on a physical level. Over time, the message and meaning she brought into my life became clear. She bought a dazzling purple electric guitar and brought it to my house to jam.

One day a few months later, Tara brought over a small vaporizer pen with a built-in glass cartridge. The cartridge was filled a white-ish orange colored sticky compound, which I recognized instantly. It was DMT. Despite having a lot more experience with psychedelics than I did, Tara had yet to try DMT. Having heard my story about how life changing it was, she wanted to try it with me. This alone was a testament to the level of trust we shared just one month into knowing each other. We meditated for a few minutes to get into the right headspace, and then I suggested she go first. She smiled at me one last time, breathed in the vapor, and then closed her eyes as she drifted away to the mystical realm waiting on the other side.

I will never forget the look of sheer amazement on her face when she coasted back down to reality a few minutes later. She had no words to process what had just happened, or where she had just gone. When trying to describe what she saw and felt, she tried so hard but just couldn't explain it. Instead, she erupted with laughter, and then cried tears of pure love and joy. The look on her face said everything. Finally, I thought to myself, someone understands!

Next, it was my turn. I had a similarly beautiful and blissful experience, and when I came back to the physical plane, we spent some talking about the absolutely incomparable, other-worldly nature of the DMT journey. After that experience together, getting in touch with the deeper levels of our consciousness, we both knew there was no way we could go back to being just friends. We had created an unbreakable bond by experiencing the most transcendent level of reality available to us as human beings. I realized that night that I loved her, and I couldn't help but wonder if she felt the same way.

The next morning, I wrote in my journal about the incredible night I'd had. When I checked my phone, there was a message from Tara that read, "Sooooo...I kinda wrote a song." She was apparently so blown away by the experience she couldn't sleep and had to journal to express her profound sense of astonishment. While journaling, she wrote a long, intricate poem and recorded a version of herself performing it spoken word style. Below her text message was the recorded file, titled "Deep Dive." I put on my headphones and pressed play. This is what I heard:

I took a deep dive, into the divine
Where infinite truth is impossible to define
Free fallin' through dimensions, transcendin' space and time
The inner workings of the universe revealed within our minds
A level of knowing, deep within my soul
We are all integral parts of an ineffable whole
My heart is cracked wide open, too much love for it to hold
Tears of gratitude stream down my face while laughter massages my soul
Vibrating so high, our energies combine
A synergistic spiral that is impossible to define
Energetic synesthesia I can almost taste the love
A frequency so palpable like an electric fuckin' hug
A deep dive into the sublime, the plunge is so divine
Reachin' for the truth deep within my soul
I can see the beauty radiate in a never endin' flow
Reality is a funny word, what does it even mean?
Once you peel back all the layers all that's left is the unseen
The frequency of love radiates within my soul
A beautiful infinity that is impossible to know
But the wonder of it all takes me places we should go

So let's take a deep dive, head first into the divine
Cuz' every day is different and who knows what we might find?
The frequency of love radiates within us all,
So just keep an open mind and let's keep nourishin' our souls

When the recording stopped, it was like snapping out of a trance! Tara's words had taken me on an inner journey through time and space. Her voice sounded so cosmic, as if Mother Earth herself was whispering secrets into my ear. It was hard to even process the last twenty-four hours of my life, and her song captured my sense of wonder and awe so beautifully. I grabbed my guitar and started composing a song of my own to express how incredible I felt.

I wrote "Come Find Me" over the span of about two hours. Feeling inspired by listening to "Deep Dive," I wanted the lyrics to reflect a sense of mystery, as well as the faith that what's meant for me will come at exactly the right time. That same feeling DMT evokes of finding what you've always been looking for, I felt I had found with Tara. I knew there were several roadblocks to our being together, especially because she lived in another state and is eleven years older than me. But I believed with my whole heart that we would be together.

2020 was a time in which almost every person on Earth experienced radical change in their lives. For me, it was a love story. I learned to fall back in love with myself, the way a child learns to enjoy the feeling of the sun, warming every molecule. I found a love so deep it swallowed me whole. It is a miraculous gift to be so supported that you have no choice but to fully believe in yourself and trust your creative abilities. In addition to her other wonderful qualities, Tara has a talent for painting. In fact, she inspired me to build an art studio for us in my basement! In the same way I've helped her embrace music, she has helped me to embrace painting and visual arts again. Our presence in each other's lives serves as reminder to give ourselves permission to create! Of course, if I had not taken the leap to play music professionally, I never would have met this amazing person who has impacted my life for the better.

"Nature loves courage. You make the commitment and nature will respond to that commitment by removing impossible obstacles. Dream the impossible dream and the world will not grind you under, it will lift you up."

—TERENCE MCKENNA

IN MY NATURE

It's in my nature, baby
to rip apart their lies
it's in my nature,
these songs can hypnotize
it's in my nature, baby
Might have to break some rules
but sooner or later
I'm gonna take ya back to school!

And as the light it changes,
the whole world rearranges,
fillin' empty spaces
hidden deep inside our mind

Found a higher power
and now has come the hour
Will you climb that tower ?
Tell the people what you find!

It's in my nature, baby
to rip apart their lies

It's in my nature,
these songs can hypnotize
It's in my nature, baby
I can't help but break some rules
But sooner or later
I'm gonna take ya back to school!

And as the light it changes,
the whole world rearranges,
fillin' empty spaces
hidden deep inside our mind

Found a higher power
and now has come the hour
Will you climb that tower?
Tell the people what you find!

Tell the people what you find!

Sing a little louder now, you are not alone
Reach a little higher now, you will find your home

"Climb the mountains and get their good tidings. Nature's peace
will flow into you as sunshine flows into trees. The winds will
blow their own freshness into you, and the storms their energy,
while cares will drop away from you like the leaves of Autumn."
—JOHN MUIR

Being in nature is a great joy for me. One day in 2018, I was
hiking alone in the Redwood Forest of northern California. I
had flown out to San Francisco to play a show at a waterfront

venue called Sam's Anchor Cafe, and while I was there, I visited and stayed with my friend Amanda. On the final day of my trip, she had to work, so I decided to book a bus tour to the Muir Woods section of the Redwood National Forest. The area was named after John Muir, an environmental philosopher, scientist, and conservation hero who worked tirelessly to protect these trees from the logging industry during the late 1800s. Driving north over the Golden Gate Bridge, I could see thousands of towering trees dotting the Pacific coastline. When I finally got down into the forest, the scenery was absolutely magical.

While walking alone down one of the trails, I stopped and sat down on the trunk of one particularly massive tree to meditate. I closed my eyes and dropped into a space of no thought, no desire, no expression—just being and listening. This moment was absent human custom and culture, a fact for which I was extremely grateful after many days spent in a crowded city. It was just me and the forest. After a few minutes, I opened my eyes, and, upon seeing the breathtaking beauty around me, I excitedly proclaimed to myself, "I'm in my nature, baby!" I was expressing the joyful feeling of existing in a natural, effortless way.

NATURAL VS. UNNATURAL

The semantic difference between the words "nature" and "natural" is very interesting to me, for several reasons. For starters, the word "natural" is derived from the word "nature," yet our society regards many aspects of nature as unnatural. In science and philosophy, arguments are made for what is natural versus unnatural. If I want to eat a mushroom that grows in the forest and shows me magical realms of beauty within my own mind that I otherwise have no way of accessing, society regards that behavior as unnatural, and even dangerous. Some would argue this state is accessible through meditation or other means, but that is incorrect. The psilocybin mushroom is a unique organism, and its wisdom can only be accessed by consuming its fruit and having the experience yourself.

Here's another interesting thing to consider. Every moment of life is considered by science to be a part of conscious reality. The only two exceptions to this are sleep and altered states of consciousness. But because sleeping and going on a psychedelic journey both significantly alter the state of the individual's mind, they must both be considered when discussing the nature of reality and the experience of human existence. Science cannot advance until we include all possible options in our search for better ways to think and live. So, to dismiss a certain state of experience as invalid not only hinders the advancement of science but also hinders our own understanding of our human experience on a personal level.

This becomes especially clear when we consider that some of the most beneficial, healing plants for human beings are demonized and discredited by modern scientific and medical communities. These vilified species include plants that have been used for thousands of years in cultures all over the world. Declaring the cultivation or consumption of certain plants and fungi illegal is simply absurd. It is both ignorant and arrogant.

Man cannot outlaw nature without outlawing a part of himself.

Arrogance is a state of mind that lays claim to an awareness born of itself, by itself, without making allowances for other intelligent factors. I find it comical reading headlines in the news such as "Scientists Think the Universe Itself May Be Conscious"... Gee, ya think? It's downright absurd to suggest that we are intelligent, and nature is not. How could intelligent consciousness evolve in a universe that lacks it? When people dismiss the psychedelic experience as devoid of any real meaning and significance, it reflects a deep lack of awareness of the simple fact that what we do not know far exceeds what we do know. However, I cannot fault those who have not had the chance to see things in this way. I was completely against the idea of eating "shrooms" when I was in college. But that's because my perspective was not informed by any real-life experience or knowledge. Like many people, I was lied to by "authorities" about what the psychedelic experience really is.

A MIRACLE OF CONSCIOUSNESS

When Swiss chemist Albert Hoffman first synthesized and began working with the compound LSD from ergot fungus in the early 1940s, it triggered a wave of psychedelic research. This included government funded studies on mental health, alcoholism, anxiety, depression, etc. LSD was found to be highly effective and was heralded as a miracle drug.

In fact, Bill Wilson, the founder of Alcoholics Anonymous, greatly enjoyed working with LSD as a medicine. But before LSD was invented, he actually got sober after being given a hallucinogenic potion that prompted a life changing mystical experience at a NYC hospital. Wilson later developed the famous and highly effective twelve-step recovery program for alcoholics. He noted frequently taking LSD with other alcoholics to help them have a spiritual awakening and said in a letter to Carl Jung that LSD "sparked a broadening, deepening, and heightening of consciousness."

"I don't believe [LSD] has any miraculous property of transforming spiritually and emotionally sick people into healthy ones overnight. It can set up a shining goal on the positive side, after all it is only a temporary ego-reducer...The vision and insights given by LSD could create a large incentive—at least in a considerable number of people. "

—BILL WILSON

Ironically enough, Dr. Hoffman himself had synthesized LSD by accident, and after ingesting it he experienced a profound state of altered consciousness. Here's how he described LSD:

"Through my LSD experience and my new picture of reality, I became aware of the wonder of creation, the magnificence of nature and of the animal and plant kingdom. I became very sensitive to what will happen to all this and all of us."

—ALBERT HOFFMAN

He later added the following statements:

"LSD wanted to tell me something. It gave me an inner joy, an open mindedness, a gratefulness, open eyes and an internal sensitivity for the miracles of creation."

—ALBERT HOFFMAN

"I was completely astonished by the beauty of nature. Our eyes see just a small fraction of the light in the world. It is a trick to make a colored world, which does not exist outside of human beings."

—ALBERT HOFFMAN

There were even articles in *TIME Magazine* highlighting the wonders of LSD and psilocybin mushrooms. A now legendary doctor by the name of Stanislav Grof made a series of videos documenting the experiences of patients to whom he had prescribed LSD for their mental afflictions. Some of these tapes are available to view for free on the internet and are quite entertaining to watch. It was clear these chemical compounds were revolutionary for the field of mental health. In fact, Dr. Grof was later quoted as saying the following:

"LSD is a catalyst or amplifier of mental processes. If properly used it could become something like the microscope or telescope of psychiatry."

This statement alone reflects what a paradigm shift LSD was for human civilization. People realized psychedelics could be used as a tool with which to zoom in on our conscious experience and create more effective approaches to mental health. Controversial Harvard professor Timothy Leary helped popularize LSD and psychedelics among young people. They started waking up to the true nature of reality and abandoning cultural tradition. This was perceived as a great danger by governments and law enforcement as they realized people were learning to think for themselves and question authority. Many of you reading this were there during the '60s or have heard about the cultural revolution that began taking place during this time. But here's some previously top-secret information you may not have known.

A CULTURE OF LIES

In the late 1960s, President Richard Nixon conspired with his closest advisors and devised a sinister plan to demonize certain psychoactive plants in the public eye. The government was facing strong backlash from the public regarding the war in Vietnam, as well as the civil rights movement. Here is a direct quote from Nixon's special counsel advisor, John Ehrlichman:

"Look, we understood we couldn't make it illegal to be young or poor or black in the United States, but we could criminalize their common pleasure. We understood that drugs were not the health problem we were making them out to be, but it was such a perfect issue for the Nixon White House that we couldn't resist it."

As if this isn't egregious enough, Ehrlichman went on to say the following:

"The Nixon campaign in 1968, and the Nixon White House after that, had two enemies: the antiwar Left and black people. You understand what I'm saying? We knew we couldn't make it illegal to be either against the war or black. But by getting the public to associate the hippies with marijuana and blacks with heroin, and then criminalizing both heavily, we could disrupt those communities. We could arrest their leaders, raid their homes, break up their meetings, and vilify them night after night on the evening news. Did we know we were lying about the drugs? Of course we did."

Let that sink in for a moment...

Governing bodies should not be telling people what plants they can or can't consume, especially when their stance is motivated by control rather than public health. It is clear these government officials were in a state of total ignorance regarding what these plants actually do for us. Frankly, those who have never experienced an altered state of consciousness are simply not qualified to make laws governing the human mind while dismissing the potential of psychedelic plants and their healing effects.

These individuals lack the direct experience of the mystical realms they are dismissing and discrediting. Forget about secondhand accounts or hours of research—each person must experience this transformative shift in consciousness on a personal level to truly understand and appreciate it. These mind-altering experiences occur directly in the present moment, as all life is lived. Those of us who have tasted this experience recognize the profound significance of these transcendent, dream-like states in which we human beings explore the inner workings of our consciousness, as well as the nature of the reality we inhabit.

"Psychedelics are illegal not because a loving government is concerned that you may jump out of a third story window. Psychedelics are illegal because they dissolve opinion structures and culturally laid down models of behavior and information processing. They open you up to the possibility that everything you know is wrong."

—TERENCE MCKENNA

Psychedelic experiences transcend our concepts of time, space, and language, and cannot be adequately explained or understood with English or any other language of symbolic terms. Music and sex are perhaps the two closest things we have to these altered states of consciousness in terms of enchantment, ecstasy, and connection. When we are locked in our lover's embrace, or dancing to the beat of the music, nothing else matters. In the psychedelic experience we feel that same attractive pull, often referred to as arousal. It is a coaxing out of one's inner motive to move forward and deepen their experience. These feelings of arousal help us focus on the importance of what is right in front of us and block out everything else. Almost invariably, something entirely new is experienced during a psychedelic journey. We encounter novelty in its truest sense.

As we move through the levels of our consciousness, new truths become knowable and accessible through the gateway of the mind. It is possible, and in fact common, to perceive a larger intelligence or awareness and make contact with other sentient entities while we are in these altered states of consciousness. To do so is extremely humbling, as I and others know very well from direct experience. It is normal to be left with more questions than answers. Who are these entities? What is the nature of this higher intelligence I encountered?

Often, these questions are written off as fantasy by those who fail to recognize the intelligence of nature. Let me be clear: These people should *not* be listened to, since they lack any experience whatsoever in the matters they are discussing. If you are someone who has experienced deep healing from a psychedelic journey, do not feel bad when someone dismisses your healing process and your positive growth. You know the truth, and no one can take your life experience away from you. Do not even be discouraged when people dismiss such notions as the spirit world or intelligent entities as silly musings. In reality, what's actually silly is denying the legitimacy of direct experience! These are real phenomena that should be studied scientifically so we can learn from them.

Instead, culturally sanctioned stories and traditions are treated as literal truth, and humankind becomes blind to the wisdom in our present moment experience. We identify with concepts of the intellectual mind rather than recognizing our role in the larger organism we are fundamentally a part of here on Earth. This kind of thinking places limits on the mind's imagination. By clinging so strongly to a certain belief or ideology, we discount the fact that we are still actively evolving into ever more complex beings by the second.

Fanaticism and dogmatism play no role in the advancement of our planet or our human society. We need open-minded, free-thinking individuals to step away from the lies and traps of our various and combined cultures and rely on their direct experiences for validation and truth about the universe. We must all venture to seek truth in our daily lives so we may contribute our piece to the human puzzle of the meaning of life. In the words of the late, great visionary scientist Terence McKenna:

"The real tension is not between matter and spirit, or time and space, the real tension is between information and nonsense."
"Personal empowerment means deconditioning yourself from the values and the programs of the society and putting your own values and programs in place."

—TERENCE MCKENNA

Legendary author and philosopher Leo Tolstoy had this to say on the matter:

"Freethinkers are those who are willing to use their minds without prejudice and without fearing to understand things that clash with their own customs, privileges, or beliefs. This state of mind is not common, but it is essential for right thinking."

—*LEO TOLSTOY*

RESETTING OUR DEFAULT PROGRAMMING

Certain psychedelic medicines—including psilocybin mushrooms—have been shown in brain scans to disrupt and deactivate the default mode network, or DMN. The DMN is commonly active when we are not focused on an immediate task in front of us. It is the self-identifying mechanism of thought which essentially runs the programs we set in our minds through habit and emotional behavior patterns. It's no wonder we are able to think such incredible, inspired, and profound thoughts with the aid of these medicines. Our quality of life depends on the quality of our thoughts, and so when people can relax enough to suddenly access their natural state of being and think incredibly profound thoughts, it is deeply healing.

Escaping temporarily from our own habitual behavior patterns provides a window of time during which one can consciously rewire their own neural circuitry. This is not a metaphor.

The best part about this exploration of our consciousness is that we can finally have an experience free of any human bias. All our lives, we have been conditioned to think and behave in certain ways by the culture(s) we grew up in. Familial culture, societal culture, national culture, and so on all set us up with an understanding of the world and our place in it, before we could come to our own conclusions.

Culture acts as a kind of filter between our minds and the direct experience of reality.

Every culture is limited by the biases of the human perspective and ignorance about nature and science. The reason we have wars over religious beliefs is because two people of different cultures cannot just accept that each has a different individual perspective on the exact same thing. It is through interfacing with nature directly that we come to know the truth. Here's another fantastic quote by Terence McKenna that sums this up perfectly:

"The truth does not require your participation to exist. Bullsh*t, does!"

If you brew a tea out of certain leaves, you get a caffeinated beverage that will stimulate your nervous system and wake you up. But if you brew certain other leaves together, you get a tea called Ayahuasca that will take you deep within the inner regions of your mind to realms and dimensions of such impossible beauty and love that you wouldn't think it was possible. But it is possible—because nature is *way* more intelligent than us. We may have invented a great many things as a species, but we did so with the mind nature gave us. We created new materials, but we did so by using the materials nature had already provided.

Do you know the reason why Ayahuasca is brewed with plants that contain DMT? It's because that particular chemical molecule is already in our body and is directly responsible for our dreams. When considering all these facts, it becomes painfully obvious that this molecule is of a high degree of significance to our biology. Through these experiences of shared consciousness with the mind of nature, we learn that plants and fungi are in fact intelligent and communicate with us. When we accept this fact, we begin to understand the world around us through direct communication with our fellow intelligent organisms. This is so crucial because the plants have a lot to teach us, and we have a lot to learn.

Ironically, even though we claim to be the most intelligent beings on Earth, we're the only creature on the entire planet that pays to exist here. Let that sink in for a moment...

Imagine a monkey having to get a job, buy a car, rent an apartment, pay bills, and work to earn enough money to buy bananas and live on planet Earth. Asinine, right? What an absurdly ridiculous thought. But that's exactly what we do. It's pretty insane when you think about it. Now imagine that monkey finds and eats a medicinal plant that helps him remember his true nature and takes him back to being a monkey for a day, and it's incredible and glorious for him. He realizes the job, the apartment, and the car are all part of his journey of growth into higher consciousness. He starts living life more fully and going after his dreams. He's happier than he's ever been. But then a bunch of other monkeys who got jobs try to tell him he can't eat that plant because it's dangerous not only to him but to society. When he tries to tell them how amazing it is, they throw him in monkey jail and tell him to stop doing drugs and that they're looking out for his best interests... Bullsh*t alert!

Misguided rules deserve to be broken. In fact, they <u>must</u> be broken if society is to advance.

Recently, I've found myself reflecting on why I enjoy breaking rules so much. I was a very rebellious child, and despite being number one in my class academically all throughout elementary and middle school, I was always getting in trouble. I often felt patronized by my teachers and was not shy in expressing when I felt I was being made to do things that were unnecessary. But I don't blame my teachers. They were simply following the rules handed down through the hierarchy of the educational system. This system indoctrinates children into a particular worldview, suppressing their natural curiosity about the nature of reality and replacing it with a story of how things are. They go on to become adults who follow rules blindly and don't question authority or even reality itself.

"If the words 'life, liberty, and the pursuit of happiness' don't include the right to experiment with your own consciousness, then the Declaration of Independence isn't worth the hemp it was written on."

—TERENCE MCKENNA

Wouldn't it be amazing if our educational system taught children to question what they experience instead of accepting whatever they are told by those in authority? Materialism and reductionist science dominate the traditional educational system and instill a point a view that depicts nature as a mechanistic, robot-like process in which inanimate particles move about by following laws. In reality, nature is very alive and very dynamic.

A few weeks after my experience in the Redwood Forest, I came across a lecture by esteemed scientist, doctor, and author Rupert Sheldrake. In it, Dr. Sheldrake essentially demonstrates how nature does not have laws, it has habits. It evolves, as evidenced by our own existence. Our minds are not ruled by laws, but by habits and patterns of behavior. We are just like nature in our continual evolution. Ultimately, we *are* nature. We grew out of this earth like a flower grows out of the ground. We must therefore accept as valid and legitimate the safe, intentional use of plant medicines. Their healing effects aid us in the exploration of our conscious ability to think in new ways and evolve.

We use certain trees to make boats in order to explore the uncharted territory of our oceans and create new pathways through our rivers. Let us also make use of certain other plants and fungi to explore the uncharted territory of our minds, and in the process create new pathways in our brain.

In this book, I've used the term "psychedelic" quite a bit. But it's important to note that not all plant medicines are psychedelic in nature. The word psychedelic was coined by Canadian psychiatrist Humphry Osmond in the 1950s, and it stems from the ancient Greek words *psyche* meaning mind/soul, and *delos* meaning to reveal or become clear. Technically, if something is psychedelic, that simply means it's revealing hidden parts of the mind and strengthening connection to the soul. However, due to propaganda from governments and media, the word psychedelic has developed a somewhat negative connotation. These plants could more accurately be described as *entheogens.*

Entheogen is a word coined by classical philosophy Professor Carl Ruck of Boston University in 1978. Ruck invented the term as a way to categorize substances that have a reputation throughout history for awakening the god within. It is a deeply profound experience to realize that God is within you, and not outside of you. This is why entheogens are so transformative and life changing. They wake you up to your true divine nature through direct feeling and experience.

By subscribing to the ideology of a religious practice or belief system, it is possible to deepen one's faith and strengthen one's relationship with God or spirit. However, nothing can take the place of a mystical experience induced by an entheogen. Many psychoactive plants have been used for centuries by various cultures and religions as sacraments to bring one closer to the divine. We need not worry that we are committing sin or upsetting God by ingesting these plants. They are here on Earth for a reason and have been providing human beings with spiritual insight for hundreds of thousands of years. In fact, many of the world's religious frameworks were developed through questions inspired by profound mystical experiences. People needed a way to explain what they saw and learned during these journeys into the realm of spirit.

We co-evolved with many of these plants through years of continued consumption, which is why every single human being has an endocannabinoid system in their body. This branch of our nervous system is equipped with receptor sites specifically built to interact with psychoactive molecules in the cannabis plant. Similarly, the psilocybin molecule in mushrooms binds directly to the existing receptor sites in our brain that stimulate serotonin production. All this to say, we should not be afraid of drugs, because we are literally made of drugs.

"All experience is a drug experience. Whether it's mediated by our own [endogenous] drugs, or whether it's mediated by substances that we ingest that are found in plants, cognition, consciousness, the working of the brain, it's all a chemically mediated process. Life itself is a drug experience."

—DENNIS MCKENNA

As I write this, several plant medicines are being tested in medical trials for the treatment of mental health disorders. The results indicated by this research are extremely promising so far, with many people experiencing a prolonged remission of their symptoms after just a single treatment. Think about that for a moment. The pharmaceutical industry has profited from making people return customers, but nature provides an actual cure. We are experiencing a worldwide psychedelic renaissance as people of various cultures wake up to the lies they have been indoctrinated to believe. The title of this book includes giving yourself permission to create your own healing. You have every right to explore your consciousness and the inner workings of your mind. If you are reading this chapter having never experienced an altered state of consciousness, let this be your permission to do so!

"I, as a responsible adult human being, will never concede the power to anyone to regulate my choice of what I put into my body, or where I go with my mind. From the skin inwards is my jurisdiction, is it not? I choose what may or may not cross that border. Here I am the Customs Agent. I am the Coast Guard. I am the sole legal and spiritual government of this territory, and only the laws I choose to enact within myself are applicable."

—ALEXANDER SHULGIN

READY TO FEEL ALIVE

———

I'm not afraid of action
I'm ready to feel alive
I'm just an animal
Tryin' to survive

I might not be stable
Livin' this kind of life
But I'm still able
To take it all in stride

Cuz I don't need to look it in the eyes
I just try to read between the lines
I'm not lookin' for the answers
To the questions in my mind

I don't mind the distance
I'm ready to make the drive
My own existence
Is startin' to unwind

Feels just like a movie

When everything's goin' fast
Sometimes I wonder
If anything will last...

But I don't need to look it in the eyes
I'm not scared of what I'm gonna find
I'm not lookin' for the answers
To the questions in my mind

Can't count how many times I've been wrong before
But I don't worry cuz nobody's keepin' score...

I'm not afraid of action
I'm ready to feel alive
I'm just an animal
Tryin' to survive

But I don't need to look it in the eyes
I just try to read between the lines
I'm not lookin' for the answers
To the questions in my mind

"The need for mystery is greater than the need for an answer."
—KEN KESEY

You know that smell certain old books have? It makes you feel like you're roaming the halls of an ancient library. It's the smell of knowledge. Sometimes I walk through the book aisle at thrift stores just to experience that smell.

One sunny day last spring, I was out for errands and decided to stop at Saver's. Resting at the edge of a stack of books on the end cap of the children's aisle was a very peculiar looking book called *Quick-Word Handbook for Everyday Writers*. It featured a picture of a cheetah, and there were several vocabulary words printed on the front cover. I thought to myself, *This would be a great tool to have for songwriting when I need a nudge in the right direction or an idea to get the ball rolling.*

Sure enough, one morning a few months later, I found myself playing guitar and noticed the book on my coffee table. The first words I saw were "able," "action," "afraid," "alive," and "animal." So, I decided to write a song based around these words. To be honest, the song flowed in a very natural way once I established a rhyme scheme and strumming pattern.

At first, I had no idea what this song even meant. I trusted, however, that my heart knew the answers. Having since played it for other people, my own understanding of what it means has expanded. Like many people, I sometimes have to talk through my thoughts out loud, either alone or with others, to understand how I'm truly feeling. This is essentially what songwriting is in a nutshell—starting somewhere, usually accompanied by an emotion evoked by the music, and seeing where it leads.

SONGWRITING AND LIFE

Writing a song requires focus. This may be obvious, but it's a different kind of focus than just playing music. When you're playing music, you're not thinking about words. You're finding a way to express yourself without them. But sometimes, the sounds you are creating evoke a particular feeling, which leads you to write lyrics to attempt to describe the feeling. Through the process of writing a song, I'm able to access parts of my psyche that are normally operating subconsciously. This allows me to derive meaning from my individual perspective, which has been informed by my individual experiences. So, despite not being able to logically make sense of the sentiments pouring out of me, I was able to create a cohesive message through the creative process of songwriting.

As human beings, we sometimes get so caught up on trying to understand the meaning of life, we forget to live it. We lose ourselves in thought instead of enjoying the wonders of life available in and around us. This song reminded me that I don't need to have all the answers to be happy or successful. If you knew how a song was going to unfold before you listened to it, the experience would be a lot less fun. The same is true in life. It's the unpredictability that makes things interesting.

A good song balances repetition and certainty while judiciously employing the element of surprise to captivate the listener.

Looking back on this song a year later, I see the message my subconscious was trying to communicate to me. Life as a professional musician certainly has its perks, but the uncertainty of not having a regular paycheck can sometimes lead to worry. This song helped me to understand my true feelings about my career path. I take everything in stride and try to live each day to the fullest. I pay attention to the synchronicity all around me, reading between the lines to discover hidden messages that illuminate my path forward in life.

So don't ask why, mystify! The purpose of art and music and poetry is to satisfy one's soul! We all grow through the act of endeavoring to understand the meaning of another soul by listening to the expression of the wisdom in their heart. The idea I'm trying to communicate here is that you as an individual are capable of bringing new ideas to the table that, at first, you yourself may not even understand. But by working through your creative expression and giving voice to your heart's inner knowing, you can create a work of art that is as concrete as it is abstract. This allows other people to create their own meaning from it, and your individual perspective then expands to become a group perspective. It is through this collective interpretation of our individual inner wisdom that society grows stronger, and humanity evolves to higher and higher states of conscious awareness.

"Life has no meaning. Each of us has meaning and we bring it to life. It is a waste to be asking the question when you are the answer."

—JOSEPH CAMPBELL

TRUTH INSIDE

———

Stand by the ocean, let the waves take me away
I ain't got nothin' much more to say
If I had another breath, I'd hold it and count to ten
I can't tell you why, I can't tell you when

Cuz life will never be the same
When you realize you've only yourself to blame
Life can never be the same
When you take away the pain and all the shame

Roll me over now but don't apologize
I can see the truth inside your lies
Take another step toward that fate of yours
Seal me in, and take my breath with but a pause

Cuz life will never be the same
When you realize you realize you've only yourself to blame
Life can never be the same
When you take away the pain and all the shame

Yes life will never be the same

When you realize you realize you've only yourself to blame
Life can never be the same
When you realize it's who you feeds the flame

"If you make it a habit not to blame others, you will feel the growth of the ability to love in your soul, and you will see the growth of goodness in your life."

—LEO TOLSTOY

This song came into being through a spontaneous late night recording session at 3 a.m. in my basement. I had been working on perfecting a new guitar chord that sounded bittersweet, almost melancholy to me. The second I got the chord progression down, I hit record and the words flowed out effortlessly in a pure stream of consciousness. When I listened back, I felt a warm energy rising in my chest, and I knew it was an instant classic. It was one of those times when you aren't trying to write a song, it just happens, organically, and with little need for conscious direction. You just surrender to the flow of the music and allow yourself to be a radio transmitting the frequency from one dimension to another.

About a week before writing this chapter, I ordered a course/coaching program online, and did not get what I had paid for. Not only was I dissatisfied with the course, but after reaching out to the person who signed me up over the phone, I was ignored and was later refused the refund I was promised would be available within sixty days should I no longer be interested in pursuing the opportunity. I then learned this person I had known as "Michael" was not even using their real name, and when I asked the creator of the program to investigate, he said there was no Michael on the team.

I felt annoyed and foolish for taking a stab at a new opportunity in a trying time, only to be treated with lies, dishonest business, and apathy. I was finding it difficult to get back to the positive attitude I cultivate on a daily basis. On top of that, I was preparing for a plant medicine retreat over the upcoming weekend and was very distracted with my disappointment in myself.

But a few days later, I happened to be on Facebook looking for music opportunities when I came across a live video my friend had posted. Funny enough, his name is also Michael, and he is the founder of True Living, a coaching and conscious business development company. The video was about self-limiting beliefs and how they shape our view of what is possible for us to achieve or create in life. Michael was reiterating that no matter your circumstances in life, it is you who defines your reality. I sent him a message thanking him for doing the video, as it was exactly what I needed to hear to help me feel better. I asked if he wanted to have a phone call soon and catch up, and we ended up talking the next day.

Michael asked what I had been up to, and I told him about being in the middle of writing this book of my songs. He loved the idea, congratulated me on becoming an author, and with excitement said, "You're never going to believe who I just spoke on stage with!"

When he told me, my jaw nearly dropped.

"Jack Canfield! The author of *Chicken Soup for the Soul!*" he said.

Not only did I know who Jack is, but I was in the middle of listening to his audiobook *The Success Principles*. It seemed like a very good omen, and I was even more convinced of that after the next words he said.

"Hey, you should come to the thought leadership and publishing summit we're hosting next month! Rick Frishman will be there. He's the guy who helped Jack publish the *Chicken Soup for the Soul* series. I'd love to connect you to each other!"

I knew immediately that I needed to follow through on this opportunity. He said he would send me the details over the weekend, so I let him know I was attending a San Pedro ceremony over the weekend and would respond on Monday. When he asked where it was being held, I told him we would be in New Jersey, south of Bloomsbury.

"No way!" he exclaimed. "I live in Frenchtown, right next door!"

The synchronicity blew me away. I told him I'd reach out after the ceremony ended. We ended up getting together for coffee that Sunday and walking around town while discussing our ideas. I discovered that not only are we both pursuing the path of conscious entrepreneurship, but we also both have a passion for plant medicines and their holistic healing powers. Michael then invited me to a conscious entrepreneurs retreat that was taking place in a few months.

"It's just outside Orlando, February fourth through the seventh," he said.

"No way," I replied. "I am already going to be in Florida just one hour from Orlando the week before. I'll see if I can change my return flight!"

When I went online to change the return date, there was a perfectly timed flight for only $39. I couldn't believe it. At this point, the synchronicity was starting to feel surreal. I did end up going to the retreat and making tons of new friends in the process.

I met a guy named Rob with whom I hit it off instantly. Rob teaches art to kids in elementary school and likes to take his sketch pad to local NYC jazz clubs at night. He also has a side business as a wedding photographer. We bonded over our mutual love of art and music, especially the power of live music to evoke brilliant artistic creations. Later that night, we played some bongos and guitar together. Despite not being a drummer, Rob sounded great and enjoyed it a lot. The next day, we took a trip to the Guitar Center store downtown to pick up a few djembes and other hand drums, as well as some shakers and percussion instruments. Later that night, we had an all-out jam session party in the big upstairs common room of the retreat center.

I met another great guy named Tony Dody, whose nickname is "The Dream-Maker." Tony and I quickly bonded, and after telling him about my book, he lived up to his name by putting me on the phone with Rick Frishman himself! I felt grateful for the chance to receive advice and wisdom from this wise, honest, and genuine legend of the publishing industry. The fact that he had helped one of my favorite authors succeed added an extra layer of synchronicity and excitement to the call. Ultimately, Rick loved my book idea and left me feeling empowered and confident about my vision.

All this perfect synchronicity and alignment would not have taken place if I had not made what I initially thought was a mistake. That action ended up putting me on the perfect life trajectory to become aware of these opportunities hidden in plain sight around me! I simply had to remind myself to stop feeding the flame so that the smoke could settle, and I could clearly see the next steps of the path I was on.

The misadventures of a professional musician's life are often long and storied. But because there's no set way that everything "should" turn out in the artist's mind, there's no problem when things don't go according to plan. These are the moments that often lead to unexpected surprises, just like the story of Write This Down. In fact, when things don't go according to plan, it's perfect fodder for more art and music. Like, "whoops, let's write a song about it!"

NOTICING AND EMBRACING SYNCHRONICITY

The more we pay attention to the coincidences and synchronicities in life, the more deeply we can perceive the higher vibrational energy in and around us. When we are distracted with self-limiting thoughts, we don't give ourselves the chance to be present in the moment and recognize the signs that are quietly showing us where to go.

There is no such thing as coincidence—only co-creation. Our choices affect and direct our lives and the lives of others. When we pay attention to the synchronicity all around us, we receive hints from the universe about what to do and where to go, and especially who to talk to or reach out to. These moments guide our decision-making process subconsciously all the time, but when we take conscious control of them, we can capitalize on the insight and direction they bring. Noticing synchronicity wakes us up to the spiritual path we have been walking all along.

Sometimes it's hard to forgive ourselves for mistakes we feel we've made in life. But as I said in the chapter on "Organic Song," you are always exactly where you are supposed to be. The universe does not make mistakes, and we can all benefit from leaning into this philosophy, especially when we are stuck in a rut because of something we did that we perceive as a mistake. Whether we realize it or not, our greatest lessons come from our greatest mistakes. But it's important to remember that a lesson is not positive or negative in and of itself. An experience can be perceived as positive or negative, but a lesson is neutral. It is the truth that comes out of the experience—the truth inside.

"Synchronicity is an ever-present reality for those who have eyes to see."

—CARL JUNG

THIS DREAM OF MINE

I took a walk to the quiet side of town,
where the ocean makes that lovely sound
Reflectin' on this dream of mine...

Lookin' back on the past and movin' on,
I'm finally feelin' a deeper sense of calm,
Reflectin' on this dream of mine...

Cuz every time I take a step back,
I see myself through another set of eyes
And it ain't hard to realize
That every misstep, every regret,
was a chance to open up my mind,
and there's no way to press rewind...

Reflectin' on this dream of mine
Reflectin' on this dream of mine

Cuz every time I take a step back,
I see myself through another set of eyes
And it ain't hard to realize

That every misstep, every regret,
was a chance to open up my mind,
and there's no way to press rewind...

Reflectin' on this dream of mine
Reflectin' on this dream of mine

Reflectin' on this dream of mine
Reflectin' on this dream of mine

I took a walk to the quiet side of town,
where the ocean makes that lovely sound
Reflectin' on this dream of mine...

"May the dreams of your past be the reality of your future."
—JIMI HENDRIX

"Who are you?" Nahko said, pulling back from our hug and staring at me with a look of bewilderment.

"I'm Nate Jones," I said with a cheeky grin.

I had just told him about how I found out I was competing against Paul McCartney for two GRAMMY Awards. I'm sure he wasn't expecting that from a random guy who snuck around the back of the venue to meet him after the concert. To be fair, I hadn't sought him out for no reason; I was on a mission that night.

I had taken my friend Ryan to see the world-famous spiritual songwriter Nahko with his band Medicine for the People.

The concert was at The Strand Ballroom Theatre in Providence. During the second half of the show, Ryan and I met an older woman adorned with beautiful fairy wings. We were all dancing around together, spreading love and good vibes to the other concertgoers. After the last song, we got to talking a bit. She was very eager to meet Nahko that night.

She had made something she wanted to give to him, and I could tell it was very important to her. I could also tell she was a very kind soul from the positive vibes she was exuding, and I really wanted to help her. Unfortunately, the show was over, and the venue was ushering people out the doors. But I wasn't going to give up that easily. Having met several artists at The Strand before, I was confident I could help her realize this dream.

"You are going to meet Nahko tonight," I said, "and I'm going to make that happen. I happen to know where the bands hang out!"

She followed me and Ryan outside excitedly, and I led us to where I remembered the tour bus being parked when I had met the members of one of my favorite bands, Third Eye Blind. However, when we turned the corner, there was nothing but construction equipment, portables fences, and rubble. She was heartbroken, and I was confused and disappointed. But I didn't lose faith. I knew the bus had to be parked somewhere along the perimeter of the venue, I just didn't know where. Ryan stayed behind with the woman while I sprinted down the street, hoping to find a clue as to where the bus might be. When I got to the end of the alley, there was a tall fence and several trucks. It looked promising, but before I could scope out the situation, a member of the venue staff saw me and yelled sternly for me to leave.

"Hey! You can't be back here, man. Show's over; go home."

Luckily, being a professional musician has taught me something about life. And that something is: The show is never over, until *you* say it is.

"Okay," I said, and walked away.

The man went back to working, but I still wanted to get a closer look. I stood on top of a trash barrel to get a better view, and jackpot!

There was the tour bus, and there was Nahko. He and his bandmates were smoking and talking while their roadies loaded their gear back onto the bus. I was ecstatic. I ran back down the street to where I had left Ryan and our new friend. But when I got there, they were gone. As I turned the other corner and headed back toward the entrance to the venue, I noticed the woman walking away. I had been gone for less than five minutes, but she must have assumed I wasn't coming back and given up.

"*Wait!*" I yelled. She turned around, and seeing the huge grin on my face, she could tell I had good news.

"I found them!" I exclaimed. "But the security guards won't let us in that way. We have to walk down Union Street."

I could tell she was skeptical, but at this point she had nothing to lose. We talked on the way down the street, and I shared my news about the GRAMMY's. She could tell I genuinely wanted to help. When we finally got to the tour bus, several other people were gathered around, and Nahko was signing autographs. I will never forget the look of excitement on this woman's face when she realized she was about to get a hug from her favorite artist. It was so satisfying to know I had helped her achieve her dream.

After their hug, she gave Nahko a bag containing seven small pieces of art she had made for him and the other six band members. It was an incredibly sweet gesture that made for a moment of love and connection between a mindful artist and an adoring fan. She explained how powerful and important his music has been in her life and thanked him for creating such beauty in the world. I took a picture and a video so she could remember the moment.

I know how overwhelming it can be to get swarmed by a rush of fans after a performance when all you want to do is relax. For this reason, I wanted to give Nahko some space. I waited until he had finished taking pictures and talking to people before asking for a moment of his time. I gave him a big hug and thanked him for his song "Great Spirit." I told him about listening to that song as well as "Budding Trees" on the day of my DMT journey and how much they moved me. I could never have known how far I would come from that day or how many people my music would reach.

"Can I tell you a secret?" I asked him. We were still locked in embrace.

"Anything, brother," he said. "What's up?"

That's when I told him I had just found out that my song "Safe as We Can" made the ballot for the 2020 GRAMMY Awards. He pulled his head back and stared at me for a good second or two, seeing the joy and confidence in my eyes. In that moment, I realized what a good decision it was to pursue my dream of becoming a rock and roll musician. Here I was, hugging one of my biggest musical heroes, and he's the one asking *me* who I am!

It was such a powerful moment for me in affirming my choice to go after what I wanted in life. I also knew that if the roles were reversed, I would feel immensely proud of the fact that my music had inspired someone else to the degree of making the GRAMMY ballot with the first song they ever released!

WHAT IS YOUR DREAM?

Several days after the quarantine kicked in, I posted a video on Facebook of myself playing a chord progression on the acoustic guitar and asked my fans to describe how it made them feel. The first four comments were all from my incredibly talented guitar student, Abby, and her family. I decided to use their responses as the lyrics of this song. The words fit perfectly and flowed like water, which is exactly how this song feels to me when I play it. I was recognizing how far I had come as a professional musician, how many people I had performed for, and how many obstacles I had overcome. It was weird to think I'd have to stop performing for a while. At that time, it was only supposed to be for a few weeks, so I decided to be productive with my time instead of worrying.

The lockdowns our world entered last year were challenging for all of us—especially artists and musicians, who thrive on community and the ability to gather and express themselves. Fortunately, the time alone and the time at home gave people a chance to reflect. Reflecting on their dreams and their desires has led many people to create amazingly thoughtful and mindful art during this time. For me, it was a chance to dive deeper into my songwriting and figure out what it is I'm really trying to do with my music. The values of mindfulness, courage, and love I hold in my heart started to appear more and more in my songs. This was the first song I wrote during the quarantine, but after it came over a *dozen* more! Each song speaks to one particular aspect of who I am, and who I hope to become. It's been a tough year for everyone, but I've found solace in reflecting on this dream of mine.

"Don't be pushed by your problems. Be led by your dreams. Enthusiasm is one of the most powerful engines of success. When you do a thing, do it with all your might. Put your whole soul into it. Stamp it with your own personality. Be active, be energetic, be enthusiastic and faithful, and you will accomplish your object. Nothing great was ever achieved without enthusiasm."

—RALPH WALDO EMERSON

ACTING OUT

Just now I thought I was real
Right then knew I had to heal
Acting out these roles we play
Time for soul to have a say, hey!

And if you ever wonder
What's out there to discover
And if you ever wonder why...

And if you ever wonder
No need to fear the other
Just take a sip and you will learn to fly

Just now I thought I was real
Right then knew I had to heal
Everything was goin' wrong
Now it's time to sing my song, go!

And if you ever wonder
What's out there to discover
And if you ever wonder why...

And if you meet your mother
Don't be afraid to touch her
Just take a sip and you will learn to fly

Just now I thought I was real
Right then knew I had to heal
Acting out these roles we play
Time for soul to have a say, hey!

"I believe that, used responsibly and in a mature way, the
entheogens mediate access to the numinous dimensions of
existence, have a great healing and transformative potential,
and represent a very important tool for spiritual development."
—STANISLAV GROF

Every now and then, an opportunity comes along in life that makes so much sense you know you can't turn it down.

One of those moments showed up in my life last summer when Tara invited me to go to an Ayahuasca retreat with her. She had just gotten off the phone with a medicine woman and musician named Eliana who hosts ceremonies in the mountains of upstate New York. This was something we had both been wanting to do for many years. I was excited, but also terrified by the mere idea of it. Ayahuasca is one of the most revered plant teacher medicines in the world, and it has a reputation for revealing truths about yourself and the nature of reality that you may not be ready to see.

I didn't think I was ready, and I was not planning on saying yes, but when Tara told me the date, it stopped me in my tracks. Friday, July 24—7/24. Anyone who really knows me knows seven and twenty-four are my lucky numbers and have been since childhood. At this point, I knew I had to say yes. It felt like the universe was winking at me, saying, "Here you go, Nate, it's time!"

So, I said yes.

My life was already pretty awesome, epic, and amazing. I was living my passion every day as a rock and roll musician, and for that I was extremely grateful. But Ayahuasca turned the tables on me and rocked my world in a way I could never have imagined was possible. As soon as I made the commitment to try this medicine, it began working wonders in my life.

At this point, I've talked a lot about the many coincidences that pop up as signs to let you know you're on the right path. Here's one that will blow your mind.

During the week prior to our retreat, we had to prepare our bodies for the medicine by detoxing from anything that could dull its effects or cause any adverse reactions. This detox is referred to as a "dieta." This meant no meat, no alcohol, no cannabis, and no processed or excessively salty or sugary foods. About five days before the retreat, I was in the kitchen making a healthy salad when I noticed a most incredible synchronicity. Sitting right on the counter, staring me in the face, was a bottle of olive oil with the name "Eliana" printed on it. I had bought the bottle several weeks prior, well before Tara had even asked me about the retreat. I was in shock at how eerie this was. If I had any lingering doubts, this obliterated them. I knew I was on the right path.

A few weeks later, the day finally came. On the way to the retreat, Tara and I decided to stop at a place called Watkins Glen Park in the finger lakes region of New York. It's a series of incredible waterfalls carved into massive stones by an ancient glacier. The views were breathtaking, and it gave us the opportunity to experience the power and magnificence of nature before working with the medicine. Later that night, we arrived and got settled. After introducing myself and making some new friends, I brought several instruments inside and put them by my mat, along with my journal and a little bottle of lavender essential oil.

BREAKING THROUGH

When it came time for the ceremony, we all laid down on our mats while Eliana played beautiful music on her guitar, singing mantras as well as her own songs. I recall feeling a sense of formless awareness all around me. It was like a foreign, intelligent entity conversing with me telepathically, offering incredibly profound messages and insights about my life path and my relationships. This entity was more like a spirit projecting itself as a maternal or grandmother type figure. My connection to my body was incredibly strong and dialed in, causing me to feel the medicine physically moving through me. As the experience progressed, I felt a growing cosmic energy, like I was in outer space or another dimension entirely. By the light of the fire from the wood stove in the room, I could actually see the glowing golden aura outlining my body. It was an unmistakable awakening to my divine nature as a vibrational being.

Eliana stopped the music for a moment and asked us all to sit up. She shared some words about gratitude and reminded us to drop into our heart space, rather than trying to analyze the experience. She then opened the door of the wood stove and spoke about how the fire is an important aspect of any sacred ceremony.

"Fire represents our life force, burning within us," she said. "In a ceremony, the fire is a symbol for transmuting old energy into something new."

"Here I have some cedar, sage, and tobacco leaves. I invite everyone to take a moment to reflect on something they are leaving behind after this ceremony. Then, one at a time, please come up to the fire and offer up your chosen herbs as a prayer. If you feel called, you can share with the group what you are letting go of."

I heard some absolutely beautiful and touching stories of growth and healing, of people letting go of things no longer serving them. When it was my turn, I had a profound realization while sitting silently in front of the fire. I can still remember this awareness rising within me for the first time.

"Today, I am letting go of the need for approval," I said.

I then shared my story about being on the GRAMMY Awards ballot with Paul McCartney.

"Wait are you serious?" someone said.

"Yes," I responded. "It's hard for me to even believe sometimes. Since then, I've been dealing with a serious case of imposter syndrome. I keep doubting my ability to produce something that will be as good as my first official song. Despite my love of music, and the fact that I've been writing tons of songs, I have this fear about recording them. I know how I want them to sound, and I've been creatively blocked out of fear of not achieving that."

I paused for a moment to reflect, and more insights came to me. At this point I was feeling the power of the medicine very strongly. My heart was opening, and I was realizing so much.

"My dad has been an extremely badass rock and roll drummer for my entire life," I said. "Ever since I started playing music, I've aspired to be as good as him, to do something he will be proud of. I realize now that what has made him most proud is knowing I am following my heart. Today, I'm letting go of the need to be good enough for myself, my family, and my friends. I'm done trying to prove myself."

A few people in the room snapped their fingers as a way of acknowledging this internal struggle we all face. It felt good to get that off my chest and release the old stagnant energy that had been holding me back. As I stared into the fire—which by the way is incredibly mystifying and cool when you have DMT flowing through your veins—I visualized my old excuses and limitations burning up. I knew there would be more challenges ahead, but I was finally ready to let go of my old struggles and face new ones. The rest of the night was amazing, and it was hard to even believe how incredible I felt.

During the second night of the retreat, we were outside around the fire pit instead of being indoors. This added a whole new level to the experience of the medicine journey and the community of beautiful people. A spiritual psychedelic experience depends greatly upon set and setting. Being outside in the very nature that gave birth to the first cells, and ultimately the human organism, was essential in helping me connect to the roots of *my* true nature. For the first time in my life, I felt like an animal in an environment rather than a person in a society.

At one point during the ceremony, Eliana played a song by spiritual heavy metal band Tool. The sheer power of the drums and guitars took me on an incredible journey. I could hardly fathom how good this band was and how powerful the vibrations of the song were. In that moment, I completely forgot who I was. For the life of me, I could not figure out what being "me" meant. I was so deeply connected to my present moment awareness that the idea of being an individual named Nate Jones was a foreign concept. I suddenly saw through the illusion of my individual persona and understood the interconnectedness of all life through direct experience. It was a classic case of ego death and rebirth.

A few minutes later, Eliana picked up her guitar and went back to singing and playing. I found myself being carried away by the melodic nature of one particular song, which is itself an ode to the great spirit of Ayahuasca. During psychedelic journeys, I normally feel very musical, and enjoy singing and being creative with sound. But up until that point, playing music was the last thing I could imagine doing. I had just forgotten who I was and felt like I had been woken up from an ancient sleep. During this song, however, I started to groove. I was loving it. *Some percussion would really take this experience up a notch*, I thought to myself. Looking to my right, I noticed my bongos. I had forgotten taking them outside. I felt an irresistible urge to play them, but I didn't want to intrude on the ceremony.

Despite my hesitancy, my intuition was telling me to go for it. In hindsight, it was probably the medicine talking. I casually reached for the bongos and slowly placed them in front of me. I glanced toward Eliana, looking for a sign that it was okay to join her, but she was deeply tuned in to the music. I then looked around the circle and saw my new friend Steve as well as a few others emphatically nodding their heads as if to say, "Yes, Nate, please smack the hell out of those bongos right now."

So, I started playing.

I came in very slowly and quietly, building up so as not to disturb the rhythm Eliana already had going. When she heard the bongos, she gave me the signal to play louder and join in. I have never had a more connected experience playing music in my life. Thought was completely out of the equation. My hands took over, and I played with total abandon while staying perfectly locked in with the rhythm of the guitar. The percussion added a kind of power to the song, and everyone was starting to sit up and open their eyes. We got quieter during the middle of the song, leaning into the moment to listen to the nuances of the music. The energy of the whole group was now present and tuned in. Then, we slowly built back up again, eventually reaching a massive crescendo before rocking out on the second part of the song.

What happened next absolutely blew my mind. At that moment, a frenzy of purging broke out. One person threw up, then another, and then another until every single person except Eliana and I had purged. When it was over, we could all feel the weight that been lifted in the circle. Everyone was smiling and happy. Incredibly, the vibrations of the drumming had facilitated the movement of the medicine inside everyone. That experience offered me a glimpse into just how powerful an Ayahuasca ceremony can be, especially when people collaborate to create music. It's not just the chemical medicine; it's also the musical medicine and the synergy of the two together.

Ayahuasca in particular is such a powerful medicine because its active mind-altering ingredient, DMT, is already inside our brains. We are simply activating our own already existing neural mechanisms.

Normally, because DMT induces such powerful mystical experiences, enzymes in our blood break it down rapidly in order prevent us from being vulnerable to a predatory attack for more than a few minutes. To brew Ayahuasca, one plant containing DMT is combined with another plant containing natural enzyme inhibitors in order to stretch the experience out over several hours. This allows a person to navigate the mystical dimension of the subconscious mind in a waking state, making conscious connections and realizations in real time. It is through these connections that we receive downloads of insight regarding our past, present, and future, which allow us to redefine our self-image and grow.

MUSICAL MEDICINE

The week after returning from the retreat, I got together with my dad to jam and noticed I was playing guitar effortlessly, maintaining complete command over the instrument. I have a feeling the Ayahuasca medicine still being in my system may have accounted for this. I was experiencing perfect musical flow. My dad was rocking out on the drums when he played the beat you hear in this song and yelled, "Just now!" as he began. He ended the beat and then yelled "Right here!" and started playing again.

My hands took over instantly as soon as I touched the guitar. I was in such a state of flow I experienced a sense of elation and connection similar to how I had felt after the ceremonies. We were grooving out in perfect harmony, and because of this, I was consciously coming up with lyrics on the spot. I thought back to that profound moment at the retreat when I forgot who I was and realized life is one big illusion: a giant magic trick orchestrated by the universe in order to experience its own essence through billions of individual perspectives, making you think you're a separate entity apart from everything else.

From this awareness, I wrote most of the lyrics right then and there, in the spirit of the present moment.

When the jam ended, my dad and I looked at each other with a mutual understanding that we had just created something badass. We began discussing the lyrics and flow of the song, and I repeated the words I had sung.

"This song's about your Ayahuasca retreat!" he joked.

We went back into jamming on the song structure again when my friend Brendan arrived. He walked in during the middle of the jam and picked up the bass, adding a nice counterpoint to the existing sounds. This allowed me to explore new melodic territory on the guitar. When I started singing again, even more lyrics flowed out. Before we knew it, we had a song on our hands. We rocked out hard for several minutes before ending the jam with an abrupt, hard stop. It felt powerful.

OPPOSITES ATTRACT

To some people, rock and roll and Ayahuasca might seem like two activities that don't go together. But while they may appear to be polar opposites, they actually have a lot in common. By playing rock and roll, we are able to exercise conscious control over the very same vibrations and electricity that power our bodies and minds. When we pick up instruments and create music on the spot, we are ushering new vibrations into the universe. This directly parallels the Ayahuasca journey in which one explores previously undiscovered territory inside their own consciousness.

By playing music, we are discovering uncharted vibrational territory through auditory exploration.

This happens not only when we write a song, but every single time we play music. Just like snowflakes, no two jams are exactly the same. Each time, we are creating never-before-heard combinations of sound. On top of that, by combining different instruments as well as human voices with each other, we add new layers to the same present moment experience. These combinations of sounds evoke many different emotions, resulting in a new personal reality for each individual listener.

There are new personal realities waiting for you inside of every song you haven't heard yet, every place you've never traveled to, every book you've never read, every person you haven't talked to, and every single plant medicine experience.

Ayahuasca showed me that there is much more of me under the surface than I consciously realized. As human beings, we are like icebergs. Our personality is the tip—the small sliver of ourselves we show to others. But underneath are all the experiences we have ever gone through, every word we've ever said or that's ever been said to us, as well as everything we've ever seen, smelled, tasted, and touched. We are not consciously aware of these influences until we make contact with the subconscious.

A healing psychedelic journey allows us to dive into the subconscious mind to process and make sense of our traumatic experiences.

Through my experience with Ayahuasca, I was provided a glimpse of what it really means to let go and trust the universe. We have nothing to fear in contacting the subconscious mind. By trusting the wisdom of our fellow organisms, we can take a deep dive into our divine nature and heal the broken parts of our psyche. Underneath all the layers of stories we tell ourselves, we will discover who we really are. This awareness has the power to liberate us from the chains of our past suffering and help us forge a new path.

"The world is not an unsolved problem for scientists or sociologists. The world is a living mystery. Our birth, our death, our being in the moment—these are mysteries. They are doorways opening on to unimaginable vistas of self-exploration, empowerment, and hope for the human enterprise. And our culture has killed that, taken it away from us, made us consumers of shoddy products and shoddier ideals. We have to get away from that, and the way to get away from it is by a return to

the authentic experience of the body...exploring the mind as a tool for personal and social transformation."

—TERENCE MCKENNA

SHAMELESS

Listen everybody I've got somethin' I got to say
Take a chance at fate and you just might find your way
Have you ever wondered if there's anything that's true?
Ain't it kinda' fun to discover the answer lies with you?

Slip inside the wheel of time and show yourself the light
Every single day you realize your future's bright
Have you ever noticed that the world is waitin' on you?
Ain't it kinda fun to learn how to make your dreams come true?

You gotta hold on to yourself
You gotta let go of the rest

Don't be afraid to ask for help
If help is what you need
Don't be afraid to try again
Cuz you just might succeed
Follow your heart and let it speak
In everything you do
Trust in yourself and spread your love
It all comes back to you...

They can't shame me, cuz this is how I feel
They can't blame me, cuz I've always been real
This moment's been comin' for so long
And I'm foldin', instead of holdin' on,
and on, and on, and on,
and on, and on, and on

They can't shame me, cuz this is how I feel
They can't blame me, cuz now it's time to heal
This moment's been comin' for so long
And I'm foldin', instead of holdin' on,
and on, and on, and on,
and on, and on, and on

"Artists are people driven by the tension between the desire to communicate and the desire to hide."

—D.W. WINNICOTT

At this point in the book, I've talked about many experiences, from highs to lows, and every moment of insight in between. But what you are about to read are by far the most difficult words I've ever had to write.

After my first experience with Ayahuasca, I was able to open up to my family and friends about a secret I had been holding in for over fifteen years. I never expected I would be writing these words down, let alone that I would have the courage to publish them in a book. Nevertheless, I believe it is important to share my story.

When I was twelve years old, a close friend of mine began to exhibit behavior that made me uncomfortable. We would play videogames, and he had a tendency to become very angry when he lost. He would take his frustration out on me, verbally and physically. We were going through puberty, and at the time, I did not understand exactly what was happening. I became conditioned to think it was normal for boys to experiment with their sexuality. I was very confused about how this behavior made me feel, because it didn't feel normal at all. I had always liked girls, and I had known that since kindergarten when I was "dating" the most kind and beautiful girl in my entire school, Hailey Joseph. As I got older, my classmates started to bully me a lot more because of my height, my glasses, my braces, and my intelligence. I didn't have many genuine friends, and so I tolerated being treated in a way I sensed was wrong because I was afraid. I was afraid if I spoke up, I wouldn't have any friends at all.

The instances were scattered at first but became more frequent and regular the older we got. I knew something wasn't right, but I was afraid that people wouldn't believe me, or they would say it wasn't a big deal. I was disgusted on the inside, but I did not want anyone else to know because I was also extremely embarrassed by it. Not only was this person one of my only friends, but he was part of the church group I hung out in regularly. I was worried I would have even fewer people to hang out with if I said anything. He was a jerk to me in middle school, constantly making fun of my height and my nerdy intelligence. He was supposed to go to a different high school than me, but when I found out he was going to be in my class again for another four years, my heart sank. On top of that, there were no girls at my high school. I went to an all-male catholic preparatory school called Bishop Hendricken.

The abuse continued throughout high school all the way up until my senior year, when I'd finally had enough. I stopped hanging out with this person of my own accord but, unfortunately, I still had to see him at school or church events. I even had to pose for prom and graduation pictures with him in the photos. Still under the impression no one would believe me, I kept the secret hidden from everyone—friends, family, teachers, and coworkers. To make matters worse, I was being bullied behind my back by the leaders of our church youth group. I believed I would always be a loser, that I would never have a girlfriend. When high school ended, I was relieved to know he would not be attending the same college.

It was not until my freshman year of college that things started to change for me. I had the courage to tell my girl-friend at the time, Rebecca, about my history of abuse. She was such a kind soul, and we had fallen in love immediately upon meeting a few weeks into the semester. Her love created a safe haven and gave me the confidence and strength to open up and let my true self shine. Rebecca was the only person on earth who knew my secret. I felt I could trust her fully, and when I did, she opened up to me about a similar thing that had happened to her with a close friend. Like me, she never had the courage to tell anyone about it. Sharing our hurts with each other helped us both immensely in sorting out old, limiting beliefs about ourselves. Unfortunately, we broke up a year later and I again felt like I had no one who understood what I had been through.

Fast forward to the beginning of 2020, a few weeks after I met Tara. In a book she was reading at the time, the author encouraged readers to re-imagine a particularly negative event from their past and essentially re-frame and replay it in the way they would have liked it to happen.

"Essentially, it's an exercise in rewiring your memory circuits," she explained.

"Cool," I thought. I instantly knew what I wanted to erase and re-record for myself. I decided to share my story with her.

Despite the fact that we had just met, I felt a deep connection with her as a friend and felt comfortable enough to share my secret. Tara was very surprised to learn this about me. I knew I didn't exhibit typical victim behaviors, at least not on the surface. I'm sure many of you who've known me for a long time are shocked to learn this about me. I felt I had done a great job since high school of letting go of the past and living with confidence. I was consciously following my dreams, rather than letting my past define me. I genuinely believed it was not affecting me. I didn't consider myself someone who had sustained trauma. Little did I know, the experience was still having an impact on my actions and my relationships.

There were many behaviors I had developed subconsciously as a way to avoid being controlled or coerced by others in any way. This manifested as me being rebellious toward teachers, coaches, and my parents. Despite being very articulate, I didn't know how to assert myself in a proper way to communicate my needs, especially in situations where I felt out of control or uncomfortable. For that reason, feelings of anger and resentment grew within me. My perspective led to negative behaviors that created even more anger and fear. I got in fights all the time at school. I was not happy about my life and was clueless to all the blessings around me.

I looked outside myself for anything that could bring me temporary happiness. I buried my emotions with video games, movies, TV, pornography, junk food, soda, and other unhealthy distractions. For years I did not see how these behaviors destroyed my health and caused rifts in my relationships. I believed I didn't need anyone but myself and would isolate for days at a time. I struggled with insomnia and was late to school so much I had to go to detention, which created even more resentment in me. It wasn't until my later teenage years that I began to take an interest in my health and fitness. I spent time correcting many of my unhealthy behaviors, but other habits still had a firm grasp on my psyche.

When college began, I used cannabis as a way to quell the negative energy within me. This incredible medicinal plant shifted my perspective in such a profound way that I became inspired to create and play and laugh. It helped me learn how to stop taking everything so seriously all the time. Around the same time, I was teaching myself to play the guitar and piano, which were very helpful outlets for relaxation. A year later I took up drumming, which gave me the opportunity to let out my physical energy and aggression in a way that was creative rather than destructive. During my senior year of college, my friend Sam and I bought a drum set and some other gear for the basement of the house we were renting. We set up the space with guitars and amps and would regularly have people over to jam. By playing music with others, I learned how to use my pent-up energy in a collaborative rather than divisive way.

I am certain that if not for cannabis, I would have struggled with my anger and resentment for a much longer time. It helped me forgive and forget. However, I eventually became so accustomed to the feelings of peace it instilled in me that I let it become a daily habit. I was sleeping in again, skipping my early morning classes, and slacking on my assignments. Looking back, I see now that skipping classes to play guitar was all part of the plan, although I didn't realize it at the time. I was still maintaining a 3.3 GPA, using my intelligence to make up for my slacking. Still, I was coasting. I was scraping by and doing the bare minimum. As my dad would say, I was carrying the lazy man's load, always taking the path of least resistance.

The only resistance I did apply in my life was learning to play music. Despite how difficult it was to play guitar and drums, my stubbornness prevented me from quitting. I was getting better and better at playing the guitar and was building confidence in the process. I followed my desire passionately and refused to give up. My spiritual journey has greatly informed my musical journey, and the two have become so intertwined that music is now a form of meditation for me. By tapping into my desire and love for music, I was able to transform my emotional pain into something beautiful.

Many of my favorite artists have done this, including Nahko. But a few months into working on this book, news broke on social media that Nahko had been accused of sexual misconduct and inappropriate behavior. When I heard the news, I didn't know how to feel. This person was one of my musical heroes who had positively influenced my life and my music. I had already typed the chapter about meeting him and coming full circle from the moment I first heard his beautiful music on the day of my DMT journey. Considering the same things Nahko was accused of had happened to me, I was distraught and unsure of how to move forward. Everyone around me was talking about how terrible he was all of a sudden. I was deeply troubled by this and unsure of what to think or how to feel.

I decided to withhold any judgment, since I was not there and did not know the full story. I wrestled for weeks with the decision of whether to keep that chapter in the book. Since I was already planning on telling the story of my abuse, I decided to keep it. I knew I could help shed light on the subject for those who are angry and confused. It would be very easy for me to boycott his music and demand that his tours be cancelled, but I am not going to do that. Regardless of Nahko's shortcomings or mistakes, the music he created and continues to create is medicine for so many people. He has been on a healing journey himself and states that in his songs.

I believe it is important to separate the art from the artist. Martin Luther King Jr. was cheating on his wife during all throughout his civil rights activism in the '60s. Does that mean we should disregard what he said in his "I Have a Dream" speech? I don't think so. Someone's mistakes should not devalue their message. The artist is merely a vessel through which creation is channeled.

I have looked deeply into the events surrounding my trauma, and I have forgiven my abuser. Looking back, I can see he was lost and trying to find his way. His family situation was very charged and tumultuous. There was always a lot of yelling and screaming at his house. This does not mean I am okay with what happened; it just means I have accepted it as a part of my journey toward love, understanding, and compassion.

Before my experience with Ayahuasca, I was walking around with an open wound that I didn't even realize I needed to heal. After going through that experience, I became aware of ways my abuse was affecting me that I had never realized before. I understand now that we are all on our own individual healing journey. I choose forgiveness. I choose not to hold onto anger and resentment over past hurts.

FOLLOW YOUR HEART AND LET GO OF THE REST

Spiritual enlightenment is not about an unending commitment to stoicism and purity. I have witnessed even the most austere monks chasing after butterflies like little children following their inner desire! The difficult thing about understanding our true desires lies in learning to recognize our needs. Many desires manifest due to needs that are not being met. Because of this, people are prone to become addicted to external pleasures and vices that do not help them advance spiritually. Desire can be extremely motivating because we want something so badly that we feel compelled to act. The distinction lies in whether we are acting out of desperation or acting out of courage. Sometimes, it's a little of both. Either way, our deepest desires are motivating every decision we make in life.

Thus, it is an illusion to think we are capable of doing or attaining something for any reason other than our own desire. No matter what our reason may be, we have used that reasoning to justify the actions we choose to take. When someone genuinely wants to grow spiritually, that wanting itself is a desire. For example, I try to help people and make them smile whenever I can because it gives me great joy. But I cannot claim I am doing it merely to help someone else, absent any personal motive. If I am helping someone, it is because on some level I wanted to do so, because I know it makes me happy. So, to assert that I am acting free of desire is not true.

This is not to say it is impossible to be selfless. Desire is present even in selfless actions. Selflessness is the state we experience when the action we are taking is flowing directly from a pure inner desire, without interference from our ego. Instead of using our reasoning mind and concluding that we ought to do something, we are operating from a place of pure intention in our heart. When I play music, I experience both the desire to create, play, hear, and feel these healing vibrations as well as the simultaneous dissolution of the self. In effect, I embody and become my desire through creative action. I know that by creating and playing music, I can bring healing to other people. But ultimately, it is my own inner desire that motivates the music I make. I am playing music because it is what I want to be doing.

The reason I'm saying all this—aside from that I wanted to—is to communicate the fact that you do not need to rid yourself of desire in order to achieve spiritual enlightenment. On the contrary, spiritual enlightenment can be realized immediately, in the present moment, by tapping into our pure and genuine heartfelt desires. This is the way children do it, and we can learn a lot from their approach. We must learn to tap into our inner child and heal old wounds. It's easy to be happy when you are not overthinking your life and your actions.

Learning to follow your bliss like a child again means you have to unlearn the behaviors you've adopted as you've grown older. You have to stop believing you are not good enough. Stop listening to the limiting beliefs and opinions of others. Stop second guessing yourself when your intuition tells you to do something or nudges you in a certain direction. Stop selling yourself short and playing small for fear of what other people will think.

I looked for happiness outside of myself for a long time before realizing it was a gift only I could give myself.

Genuine desire does not concern itself with the judgments and opinions of others. It is focused solely on our own enjoyment, on deepening our understanding and developing our unique individual perspective in life. Just as a child wanders off into nature, following the innate curiosity stimulated by the unknown, we can learn to pursue our desires naturally without the pressure of being right or wrong, of succeeding or failing. Success and failure are false concepts that delude our thinking. Instead, this new perspective and approach allows us to achieve lasting inner peace by living joyfully in the present moment.

> *This is what true spiritual enlightenment looks like—living free of guilt and shame and stepping into our power of personal alchemy and transformation.*

In this book, I have shared the highs and lows of my life's journey. There have been many incredible and beautiful moments, but there have also been some painful moments. It's easy to want to remember the good moments and forget the bad ones, but that is not how we grow. Without the struggles and suffering I have been through, I am certain I would not be who I am today. The pain I have experienced has taught me how to love others, how to love myself, how to respect all beings, and how to enjoy the journey of life for all its ups and downs.

Notice how I did not refer to myself using the word "victim" in this chapter. This is because I do not think of myself as a victim. Did I sustain trauma? Yes. But does that mean I am a victim? Only if I choose to look at it that way. The words we identify ourselves with are powerful. Looking back, I wouldn't change a single second of my life. It's all led me to this moment, writing these words in what will be one of the final chapters of my book. We all have a story, and that story would not be complete without every single thing we've ever experienced. But it's up to *you* to decide who you are, not anyone else. Don't be afraid to give yourself permission to create your own healing!

"When you look back at your own life, you see...the sufferings you went through, each time you would have avoided it if you possibly could. And yet, when you look at the depth of your character now, isn't a part of that a product of those experiences? Weren't those experiences part of what created the depth of your inner being? Suffering is part of our training program for becoming wise."

—RAM DASS

RIVER OF LOVE

Floatin' on a river of love,
carry my songs to distant shores
Floatin' on a river of love,
there's more to life than you could possibly explore
On this river of love
this river of love

I talked too much about things that didn't matter and
led nowhere,
Cuz I was scared, so very scared
I acted tough, tryin' to climb a ladder that led nowhere,
Cuz I was there, already there

Floatin' on a river of love,
carry my songs away to distant shores
Floatin' on a river of love,
I know you'll see what I've been searchin' for
On this River of love...
This river of love...

I'm takin' my time, doin' it right,
Rememberin' all my teachers
There's somethin' inside, shinin' a light,
It's flowin' through my speakers
I'm takin' the blame, for all of the pain
I've been feelin' lately
There's nothin' to say, it's all in the way,
that you play

Floatin' on a river of love,
Carry my songs to distant shores
Floatin' on a river of love,
There's more to life than you could possibly explore
Floatin' on a river of love,
Carry my songs away to distant shores
Floatin' on a river of love,
I know you'll see what I've been searchin' for
On this river of love

"Man is a stream whose source is hidden. Our being is descending into us from we know not whence."

—RALPH WALDO EMERSON

It was Halloween night, and I found myself standing atop a giant rock in the middle of the desert, surrounded by an enormous drum circle. Situated atop a large red clay plateau called Cathedral Rock, over fifty different drummers were playing a mix of bongos, djembes, and hand drums. Some had flutes and rattles as well as other smaller percussion instruments. Dozens of people were dancing ecstatically to the complex rhythms while howling up at the moon. The experience was so surreal; it felt like a scene out of a movie.

How did I end up here, you ask? Well, it all started when Eliana invited me and Tara to join her and some other people from our medicine tribe who were flying out to Sedona, Arizona. She assured us it was a magical place that felt like heaven on earth. She was right.

Sedona is one of the most spiritually charged places in the entire world. Tara and I spent five days there, and even the woman I spoke to at the National Parks department was eager to tell me about "the energy vortexes." Apparently, the vortexes are several areas of land in Sedona where the spiritual energy is said to be higher, or at least more concentrated. This may sound a bit out there, but almost every store you enter has a map of where the vortexes are located. Thousands of people gather nightly to watch the sunset at one particular vortex located near the airport. Despite being a very open-minded person, I was skeptical of such claims until I felt it for myself. It was unmistakable. Native Americans, including the Navajo and Hopi people, settled on this land long before the town of Sedona was built, and for good reason.

But let's get back to the story. Tara and I had hiked up Cathedral Rock during the day, and we were mesmerized by the incredible views of the Arizona desert. Staggering red rocks jutted out from the otherwise flat landscape in every direction we looked. There was definitely a sense of magic in the air as we got closer and closer to the top. The gorgeous trails were lined with many different colored cacti and juniper trees growing in twisted spiral patterns. Upon reaching the summit, we were met by one of the most amazing sunsets I have ever witnessed. The light was refracting and creating beautiful auras and orbs in our visual field. We lingered there for about an hour, taking pictures and soaking in the beauty.

On the way back down, we began hearing what sounded like drums, but could not see the source of the sound. Dusk was starting to settle in as we rounded the corner to the final descent. That's when we noticed the enormous drum circle happening below! There had to be at least seventy to eighty people already gathered.

As we climbed back down the mountain, the number kept growing. When we finally reached the plateau, there were hundreds of people celebrating the full moon. One guy was juggling glow-in-the-dark bowling pins, someone else was spinning fire, and almost everyone was dressed up in a Halloween costume. We spent the next few hours there meeting people, dancing, singing, and playing several different drums and bongos. Sometime around midnight, Tara and I were just about to leave when I was handed a guitar by someone I didn't even know. He not we had just played a Neil Young song while I sang the words.

"My name's Kenny!" he said.

"Nice to meet you, Kenny. I'm Nate, Nate Jones," I said.

Kenny was an older gentleman with long gray hair.

"You have a wonderful voice, Nate, would you play us a song or two?" Kenny asked.

At this point, I glanced at Tara and noticed a look of amusement on her face. We both knew there was no way we would be leaving any time soon if I started playing the guitar. But when given the chance to extend this beautiful evening with beautiful music, we knew we had no choice but to stay.

I played my song "Write This Down," and people were completely blown away by it. As soon as I began singing, a circle started to form around us. The song lasted nearly ten minutes, as we kept repeating the choruses, clapping and howling at the moon and stars. Soon a few more people joined in with drums and the circle grew larger. The music was transformative. I was walking around the circle with the guitar, giving each person the chance to sing the chorus with me. When it was finally over, people requested more, so I played "Organic Song." That was another hit with the crowd of spiritual music lovers who had gathered. Everyone started singing along, just as the lyrics say.

Someone then asked me to play "Stairway to Heaven," which I happily obliged because it is one of my favorite songs of all time. I gave it my best Robert Plant, howling into the vast expanse of the desert night with powerful conviction. When that was over, some light conversation broke out as people in the newly formed circle started introducing themselves to one another. During this break in the music, I was approached by a man named Rafael, who introduced me to his friend Rogger. They both spoke Spanish, so we conversed bilingually for a little while. Rogger and Rafael were showering me with love and gratitude for the songs I shared.

"You have something special, my friend," Rafael said. "I see it in you, and I feel it in your voice. Amazing musician!"

"This is beautiful soul music my brother. Thank you!" Rogger added.

I felt so much love in that moment. Their words made me feel appreciated, valued, and happy that I could create such a deep musical experience for them. The loving energy of the people of Sedona had filled me with peace and joy. There was so much love in the air, I decided it made sense to share one last song with everyone—"River of Love."

I sang my heart out and left nothing on the table in my performance. Combined with the palpable energy of the vortex, and the moon glowing brightly overhead, the song carried us all away into a state of pure love and unity. Everyone in the circle linked arms and swayed back and forth, singing this powerful song with me. It was a moment of deep, ecstatic bliss.

After the song was over, I returned the guitar to Kenny and sat down with Rogger and Rafael to enjoy some cannabis and unwind. Rogger asked me how I write songs, where the words come from, and what inspires me. I told them my approach is to "channel the messages I am receiving from source and build a new musical reality in the present moment."

I discussed how we use the word spell in the English language, as I mentioned in the "Tip of Your Finger" chapter.

"The idea that songwriting is magic becomes very obvious once we understand the way we create meaning through organized sound and language," I said.

This was a novel concept to both Rogger and Rafael, and they expressed their gratitude for my explanation of how I understand the creative process of songwriting.

"It's like painting for me," Rogger said. "I just trust my inner vision and let my hands move naturally to see what spirit wants me to create."

"Exactly," I said. "You just have to be open to the flow, like a river. You step into the stream of consciousness and see where it takes you."

At this point, Tara had joined a circle next to ours and made friends with a couple named Zach and Moshe (pronounced Mo-shuh).

"I just met your two biggest fans!" she exclaimed. "Besides me, of course."

"We love your music!" Zach said.

"Yes, amazing songs and your voice is so soothing," Moshe added.

I thanked them both for their compliments and stood up to meet them. We hit it off instantly and decided to hike back down to the parking lot together and find somewhere to eat. Zach and Moshe told us they were staying at a place called Angel Valley, and recommended Tara and I check it out. A few days later, we got the opportunity. The grounds were decorated with several labyrinths, beautiful statues and wooden art pieces, tons of meditation spots, and a beautiful river we were lucky enough to swim in. It was a chance to decompress and drop into our hearts after a wild and unforgettable journey.

Sometimes, the universe will send you an unexpected gift. The writing of this song was one of those times. To be completely honest, it just popped into my head one day while I was practicing guitar and singing through my sound system at home. I was reflecting on my love for Tara, thinking about how much my life had transformed because of meeting her. I knew her love could not have come into my life if I had not first cultivated that loving energy within myself. My mind had acted as a magnet, attracting that which resonated harmoniously with the loving vibrations I was already emitting.

THE RIVER OF LOVE

A river is one of nature's most essential functions. It is not an entity in and of itself but is instead formed by the energy of multiple forces in nature. "River of Love" flowed into my mind, just like water flows downstream. That day, I was lucky to have my net set up to catch the magic!

We are all afloat on the river of love that is life, moving downstream from our source with each new generation at the forefront. We are all supported by the universe at every moment of life with enough resources to exist and experience life on earth. Rivers carry essential resources from one place to another. In this same way, songs pass from the realm of imagination to the realm of audible reality to transmit meaningful messages that lead to the expansion of consciousness. We often don't recognize just how supported we are by this river of love. It is in us and around us all the time, even if we are not consciously feeling it. In order to tap into the creative potential of our being, we just have to go with the flow, like a river.

"We are all just walking each other home."

—RAM DASS

THE LAYERS OF YOUR SELF

I tried to tell you the truth
You did not want to hear
You said you needed proof
I said it was quite clear

You've got to feel, your wealth
You've got to steal, your health
You've got to live, in stealth
You've got to peel, away, the layers of yourself

You've got to peel away
the layers of yourself

You said you wanted to try
I said it's taken me lots of time
I'd think you'd be surprised
To learn you're more than the average guy!

You've got to feel, your wealth
You've got to steal, your health
You've got to live, in stealth
You've got to peel, away, the layers of yourself

You've got to peel away
the layers of yourself!

"Spiritual intelligence is the capacity to conduct our life in such
a way that it reflects deep philosophical and metaphysical
understanding of reality and of ourselves discovered through
personal experience during systematic spiritual pursuit."
— STANISLAV GROF

Remember that line in "River of Love" about remembering all my teachers? Well, it's a reference to my experience at my first San Pedro plant medicine ceremony. San Pedro is another name for the cactus echinopsis pachanoi, which grows in several South American countries, including Peru and Ecuador. It has been used for thousands of years as a medicine to help open the heart and reconnect people to their love and understanding. The original indigenous name for the cactus is Huachuma, but there is a very interesting reason why the Spanish began referring to it as San Pedro. They likened the profound experience this medicine induces to being at the gates of heaven. In Christian mythology, Saint Peter is the one who greets you at heaven's gate after death. The medicine is known for showing you the ways in which you are not living in truth and love and helping you see how you can live in deeper alignment with your values.

After my profoundly healing experiences with Ayahuasca, I was curious to try this medicine as well. On the day of the ceremony, I wore a tunic style shirt I had gotten at Blue Cliff Monastery. Printed on the front of the shirt was a circle, inside of which read the words, "Enjoy the present moment." I mentioned to our ceremony leader, Carolina, that it was a piece of calligraphy done by Thich Nhat Hanh. She and her partner Shane were familiar with his work and teachings and were happy to know I had been on a journey of mindfulness and peace prior to trying plant medicine.

After the ceremony began and we drank the medicine, everyone in the room was beginning to feel their hearts opening up. People shared stories about the heartbreak in their lives, the hurts they'd experienced, the loves they had lost. I shared some deeply personal stories from my own life, including how I always feel the need to improve myself. No matter how successful I become, I still feel the need to prove myself to family, friends, and ultimately, to myself. Having been bullied, I was very aware of the struggles of those around me, and I wanted to be everyone's hero and savior.

This turned into a conversation where I revealed something I've been embarrassed about for several years. I admitted to the group that despite being a spiritual, mindful person, I rarely meditate. I find it hard to sit and relax.

"There is a restlessness within me that I usually satisfy by playing music," I said.

"Remember Nate," Carolina said, "while playing music is a beautiful form of meditation and connecting with your heart and your mind, it cannot take the place of silent meditation. You have to be okay with yourself, to be able to sit and feel whatever comes, and accept it, and practice. That's why we call mindfulness a practice, right? Because it's not easy, but you get better."

I knew she was totally right. Through our group discussion, I realized my difficulty in sitting with myself stemmed from my beliefs about not being good enough. I always felt there was something I needed to accomplish instead of just enjoying a moment of silence and peace.

Sensing I was in need of some deep healing, Shane and Carolina started gathering blankets and pillows, creating a makeshift bed for me to lay on. They instructed me to lay down on the floor in the middle of the circle so I could absorb the healing energy of the group. Carolina covered me with more blankets and put a bandana across my forehead which covered my eyes. She also placed essential oils including lavender and eucalyptus on my wrists and my temples.

Carolina then began to sing several icaros. An icaro is a medicine song a shaman sings to invoke the healing properties of the plant spirits in the medicine. Next, Shane began to shake his rattle in a repeating, hypnotic pattern. As Carolina chanted, my entire body began to vibrate in a way I have never experienced before. She was simultaneously brushing my skin and clothes with a sacred healing wing of bird feathers and repeating her icaros and mantras. As she scanned different parts of my body, she would stop and focus on particular areas. Each time she did this, the sensation of vibration increased. I felt waves of loving energy wash over me as I laid there motionless in a state of total relaxation. It felt like I was back in the womb, completely supported and receiving incredibly nurturing and healing energy.

The entire experience lasted probably twenty minutes, but it seemed to go on for hours. When she finally stopped, silence filled the room. Without moving a muscle, I laid there, still in disbelief over what I had just felt and experienced. I didn't even want to get up. I wanted to lay in that stillness and bliss forever. A few more moments passed as we all breathed deeply into the silence. I still vividly recall the words I spoke next.

"Well...," I said to the group, my eyes still covered with the bandanas, "I really thought DMT was going to be the craziest thing that ever happened to me...but I was wrong."

Everyone laughed at my remark, which helped to relax the intense atmosphere in the room.

When I finally sat up, Carolina looked at me with a surety that was comforting and encouraging. I stared deeply into her eyes without looking at a single other person, not even Tara. I realized I had been putting the healing of others before my own healing. I felt the shame of not honoring myself and my practice of mindfulness, but I also felt a sense of self forgiveness that wrapped me in a warm embrace. Carolina instructed me to pray for Thich Nhat Hanh, to honor his sacrifice and his teachings by living the practice of mindfulness.

At this point, I felt the overwhelming urge to go outside. Not only that, but I wanted to feel the earth on my feet, so I didn't even put on my shoes or socks. We were at a cabin in the forest, and there was a very large, steep hill behind the house that I couldn't even see the top of. It was nearing sunset, and as I looked up at the sky, I felt my intuition telling me to climb. With my hands against my chest in prayer position the entire time, I walked all the way to the top of the hill barefoot. Despite it being forty-five degrees outside, I was not cold. I was breathing deeply and shedding tears of pure gratitude for the healing I had received.

My lack of footwear forced me to be very mindful of where I stepped, which helped me stay focused, just like in walking meditation at Blue Cliff. As I walked, I kept Thich Nhat Hanh in my heart, reflecting on his enormous sacrifices and loving compassion for everyone, including his enemies. At just twenty-nine years old, he had been exiled from his home country of Vietnam for peacefully protesting the ruthless genocide of his people. Occasionally, I would turn around and look back at the cabin, knowing I was going to keep walking until I reached the top. I was reflecting on how difficult it must have been for my teacher to walk away from his homeland while his people were being oppressed and murdered. It put everything in perspective for me. Holding this loving awareness in my mind, I pressed onward.

When I reached the top, I saw the most beautiful sight my eyes have ever beheld. The sun was peeking through the clouds, casting its incredible golden, shimmering light on a meadow of tall grass. All sorts of insects, from butterflies to bees to dragonflies and mosquitoes, seemed to be dancing up and down in the beams of light. With my hands still in prayer position, I stepped up onto a mossy log lying on the forest floor and began to meditate. I basked in the radiant sunlight of that moment, allowing its energy to warm me from the inside and outside. I took deep, rejuvenating breaths and felt an incredible sense of peace and well-being come over me.

Suddenly, I heard a fairly loud noise within a few yards from me. It sounded like a small animal taking a few steps. When I opened my eyes, I didn't see anything, so I went back to meditating. Not more than two seconds later, I heard a much louder noise and realized there was a very large animal moving quickly toward me. When I opened my eyes that time, I was relieved to see it was only a deer. She stopped about ten feet from me as if to also take in the magical scene of the meadow, before scampering away with a few graceful bounds.

I could not help but feel the obvious connection between this moment, and the moment with the mother deer at Blue Cliff. It was as if the deer was a symbol of my returning home to the practice of mindfulness and the peaceful stillness in myself. It felt like a rebirth. I stood there for another few minutes, taking in the sheer beauty of the scene, and feeling incredibly grateful for my life. A few moments later, Shane came running up the hill looking for me, almost out of breath. Apparently, I had been gone for almost half an hour! As we walked back down the hill together, I couldn't believe how far I had climbed. It proved to me just how capable I am of achieving difficult tasks when I'm in the right mindset, trusting my intuition and my inner power.

Once I got back to the house, everyone welcomed me with open arms. Despite my feeling of rebirth, I didn't feel like a different person. I felt like a stronger version of myself. I felt recommitted to my purpose, which is one of peace and compassion. When we reconvened the circle, I proceeded to sing my heart out during the musical portion of the ceremony. It felt so good to play my songs for everyone and to really let my heart sing its truth. I felt accepted for being exactly who I am in that moment. When the music was over, Tara wrapped me up in her warm, loving embrace and reminded me I am exactly who I need to be. All the layers I had built up from trying to be perfect had fallen away.

After my San Pedro experience, I was filled with a deep awareness of my heart's ability to expand, grow, and express its feelings to my conscious mind. I came away with a stronger commitment to my purpose in life.

It is my mission to create incredible, life-changing music that helps people remember and wake up to their true divine nature so they can heal themselves and radiate positive energy.

I started to realize how simple it really is to just be yourself and follow your heart. There's a lot less to think and worry about when you trust your intuition and act in the way your heart tells you is right. It really takes a lot of the guesswork out of life! But in order to do this, we have to let go of the labels and limits we've imposed on ourselves. The truth is hard to find when we are distracting ourselves with thoughts of who we're supposed to be. Through our present moment awareness, we can peel away the layers of the self and access the divine within.

"We have been to the moon, we have charted the depths of the ocean and the heart of the atom, but we have a fear of looking inward to ourselves because we sense that is where all the contradictions flow together."

—TERENCE MCKENNA

MAKE IT LAST

Make it last, make it last, don't live too fast
It's not about the money
Universe so vast, no future no past,
Live now honey
Rock and roll is makin' its way back,
and it feels kinda funny
You can find a way out if you shed your doubt
the skies are sunny

I don't need no heroes or enemies,
I just need the stars in the sky
I just wanna see what's in front of me,
no need to look behind
I don't need no heroes or enemies,
I just need the stars in the sky!
I just wanna see what's in front of me,
don't matter how or why!

Well they know who you are
and they're comin' to find ya
that white light in the sky

will someday blind ya
well they know who you are
and they're comin'... to get ya...
they're comin' to get ya!

I don't need no heroes or enemies,
I just need the stars in the sky
I just wanna see what's in front of me,
No need to look behind
I don't need no heroes or enemies,
I just need the stars in the sky!
I just wanna see what's in front of me,
Don't matter how or why!

Make it last, make it last, don't live too fast
It's not about the money (yes it is)
Universe so vast, no future no past,
Live now honey (here it is)
Rock and roll is makin' its way back,
And it feels kinda funny (doesn't it?)
You can find a way out if you shed your doubt-
The skies are sunny (this is it)

"Hurrying and delaying are alike ways of trying to resist the present."

—ALAN WATTS

In May of 2021, Tara and I hosted a three-day retreat in the rainforest outside of Asheville, North Carolina. Yes, you read that correctly, there is a temperate rainforest in the middle of North Carolina! It's called the Pisgah National Forest, and the energy there is quite wonderful and refreshing. We booked a house on Airbnb tucked away in the mountains just south of the city. Among the attendees were one of Tara's coaching clients, Rebecca, as well as my friend Kevin, whom I met at Blue Cliff. We focused on mindfulness techniques, nature, meditation, and music/sound healing. It was an incredible experience that brought a lot of group healing and affirmed our desire to host more retreats in the future.

A few days after we returned home, I was browsing retreats online and came across a ten-day shamanic rebirth program on the big island of Hawaii. The name piqued my interest on its own, but the location added a layer of synchronicity. Kevin had just returned from living on the big island and had been encouraging me to go there for several months.

The program was fairly expensive, but despite the steep price tag, my intuition was strongly nudging me to call the retreat center and find out more information. So, that's exactly what I did. When I called, a woman by the name of ZZ answered. I expressed my interest in attending but told her I wasn't sure if I could afford the full ten-day program. She happily informed me that we could build a mini program with just a few of the activities, one of which was an evening ceremony with a special psychoactive Hawaiian plant medicine. I was very curious but felt I needed a bit more information. When she asked what I do, I told her I was a professional musician working on a book about music, creativity, mindfulness, and plant medicine.

"I'm always looking to learn new things about the universe and deepen my understanding of my purpose in life," I said to her. "I'm curious to learn more about shamanism because I've experienced some incredible insights from my recent plant medicine journeys."

The next words she said completely changed the way I look at life.

"Well, actually, shamanism has nothing to do with plants."

"Wait, really?" I asked.

"Yes," she said. "A shaman is a person who has healed themselves and can heal others, both physically and spiritually. A true shaman can walk between worlds and communicate messages from the spirit realm. Our shaman Jack, a.k.a. 'Chief Golden Feather,' was trained by the Lakota Native American tribe."

"Wow," I said. "I had always associated shamans with plant medicine and psychedelics, but you're saying the two are separate? I've believed in the spirit world ever since I did DMT, but it's hard to know what's real and what's my imagination."

"Yes," she said. "Keep in mind, Nate, nothing real can be threatened, and nothing unreal exists."

I had to pause for a moment to think about what this meant. As I processed her words, I felt a sense of freedom and elation wash over me. This was exactly the sort of wisdom and insight I had hoped for when I picked up the phone to call. At this point, I knew in my heart that we needed to take this trip, and I felt strongly that it had to happen before I finished my book. I envisioned this experience being a final source of inspiration to round out the stories and lessons in my chapters.

So, I gave myself permission to create a spontaneous last-minute vacation to a tropical paradise!

MINDFULNESS IN ACTION

The trip was an absolutely life-changing journey during which I discovered some incredibly interesting things about myself. For starters, I realized just how strong my mindfulness muscle has become. This became apparent during a series of frustrating travel interferences and delays that deeply tested our patience. For starters, our 7:30 a.m. departing flight was canceled and replaced with a 6 a.m. flight just three days before our trip. Then, the new flight was canceled right as I was getting into bed at 10 p.m. the night before. After an hour on the phone, the best the airline could do was put on each on three separate flights to Hawaii, with Tara arriving four hours later than me. "Frustrating, but at least we will still get to Hawaii tomorrow," I thought.

I went to bed and got up 3:30 a.m., only to learn that our scheduled Lyft driver had cancelled the ride. At that point it was too late to find another ride, so we had no choice but to drive an hour to Boston and leave Tara's car unlocked in the parking garage so her dad could pick it up. On the way to the airport, I called the airline and got them to find a way to at least put us on the same flights, still four hours late, but at least arriving together. We flew to Miami with no problems, but when we got there, our new flight crew hadn't even arrived at the airport. When we finally did board the plane, we then sat in the runway for over two hours because they were waiting for "beverages" for the flight. Because of this, we missed our connecting flight in Phoenix. We were put on a series of later flights now set to arrive in Hawaii at 9 p.m. instead of 2 p.m. I was annoyed and exhausted but still maintained a positive attitude, feeling grateful to be going to Hawaii.

However, while waiting for this new flight in the bathroom, my phone got another update that the flight had been canceled. I tried to remain calm, but knowing I was alone, I let out a yell of frustration to vent my feelings. I then waited in the customer service line for forty-five minutes trying to get a new flight. They said we would not have time to make it to Hawaii that night and would need to get a hotel in Phoenix. When I asked if that would be paid for by the airline, they said no. *Seriously?* I remember thinking to myself, *What a nightmare travel experience this is.* But then I thought twice, and realized we were safe, no one was hurt, and the only thing we had lost was time. It was far from a real nightmare.

As I relaxed, I overheard the agent next to ours tell a woman in line she could put her on a different airline's flight to San Francisco at no cost, which would allow her to catch the last flight to Hawaii from there. I promptly found the flight she was talking about and showed my phone to our agent. She gave it a try and it worked! But the layover time was only thirty-nine minutes, and the next flight was in an entirely different terminal that required a tram ride across the airport. Both Tara and I managed to stay mindful the entire time, reminding ourselves we'd be in Hawaii soon enough and forget all about our travel woes. We had to sprint across the airport with all our bags, but we treated it like a race and miraculously made it with only three minutes to spare!

When we finally arrived at the airport in Hawaii, I started to relax a bit as I felt the refreshing island breeze caress my skin. I could hear the leaves of the towering palm trees that dotted the airport parking lot rustling in the wind. At this point, I had let go of the frustrations of our very long travel day and was relieved to have finally arrived in Hawaii.

But when I got off the shuttle to pick up our rental car, the universe had one final test for me. The woman at the desk informed me she had to charge my card 500 dollars as a security deposit for the car, despite the fact I'd already paid for it. I knew this hold was going to make it very difficult to have any spending money while there. Since it was the only way to get the car, I agreed to the charge, but my card was declined by fraud protection. Next, she told me she actually couldn't even rent the car to me because I was apparently on a do-not-rent list. I had no idea how this was even possible considering I had only rented a car in my own name one time a few years prior with no issues. At this point I was so exhausted and delirious I started to laugh out loud. Tara was able to put the car in her name, and I went outside to chill out.

While I was outside, I noticed a guy who had been on our very first flight from Boston that morning and started chatting with him. His name was Natto, and he was from Oregon. I took note of the synchronicity of him being on our earlier flight and having an extremely similar name to me. Tara then came outside and handed me the keys, smiling excitedly.

"They gave us a Camaro!" she said.

I was expecting some basic economy car, so this was a nice surprise after our day of hassles.

"Sweet ride, dude!" Natto said as I pulled the car up.

"Thanks, man. Hope you have a great vacation!" I said as we drove away.

A WHOLE NEW WORLD

When we finally arrived at our Airbnb room, it was 12:30 a.m. Hawaii time, which was 6:30 am Eastern time, twenty-seven hours after we had left the house. Needless to say, we were exhausted. I was hoping the island vibes and nature would relax me as we drove from the airport to the room, but because we got in so late, it was pitch black outside. In a way, however, it was perfect, because the next morning, we woke up to an absolute paradise.

The room we booked was at a retreat center/conscious living community called Sundari Gardens. The pictures looked amazing online, but we had no idea just how vast and beautiful it would be. The sun woke us up at 5:30 a.m., so we went outside to explore. There was a thin layer of morning mist hanging in the atmosphere, while the sounds of all sorts of exotic birds and insects decorated the airwaves. The land included several colorful buildings, an organic permaculture food forest, and even an outdoor yoga gazebo overlooking the ocean. Everywhere I looked were colorful exotic plants and ancient looking trees adding vibrancy to the land. There was even a rainbow eucalyptus tree. Most importantly, though, we made great friendships with the genuinely awesome and interesting people living and staying there.

That evening, we were invited to a sacred song circle at the volcanic hot ponds just after sunset. When we showed up, it was pitch black, and all we could hear was the roar of the ocean just a hundred feet away. However, we noticed a faint light flickering in the distance. We trusted our instincts and walked toward the light. As we got closer, we could hardly believe our eyes. There were at least forty people, and everyone was butt naked, singing together by the faint candlelight. Tara and I looked at each other and burst out laughing. Realizing we were overdressed for the situation, we decided to take our clothes off and join the party!

I shared some of the songs I had written, as well songs from the plant medicine community and some mindfulness songs I'd learned at Blue Cliff. It was a wonderful experience of community and non-judgment. The entire evening had a very free-spirited nature to it. It was now clear to me that Hawaii was not only a tropical paradise in terms of the natural beauty and breathtaking landscapes. The people living here were exactly the kind of people I wanted to connect with.

The following evening, our trip took an even more interesting turn. I had emailed Christine, the owner of Sundari, after we booked our stay and was able to set up a concert for the Friday night. About fifteen to twenty people attended, and it was a massive success that ended in a giant dance party. I played some of the popular medicine songs we all knew, as well as many of my original songs from the earlier chapters of this book. "River of Love" was a crowd favorite, as was "Make it Last."

I also played "Write This Down" and told the story of how I got the mushroom chocolate that later inspired the writing of that song. Everyone enjoyed the story and the synchronicity. At one point during the show, I noticed a woman we had just met hand something to Tara, but I quickly forgot about it. I was completely tuned in and focused on the music, the audience, and the vibes we were co-creating. After the show, I received some incredible feedback on my music, but my favorite was from a girl named Kai. We had met the day before in a workshop she facilitated called "Divine Play."

"Your music is so beautiful and rich. It's empowering and gentle at the same time," she said, before pausing briefly to think.

"Your songs have this simple consistency, but then your voice does these exciting things that make me go, 'Wow!'"

"That's awesome to hear!" I said. "Can you tell me more about what you're noticing in my voice and why it's exciting to you?"

She paused again, searching for the right words to capture her feelings.

"It's like your song structure and melody is the trunk of a tree," she remarked, "and then your lyrics are these long, intricate branches that stick out in different directions, and the sounds your voice makes are like the beautiful exotic fruit that tastes amazing and nourishes you."

"Wow!" I exclaimed. "That's an incredible analogy. I'll be thinking about that for the rest of my life!"

After the concert, Tara and I headed back to our room to unwind and get ready for bed. When we arrived, she stopped me, saying:

"Oh! I almost forgot to tell you... We got a mushroom chocolate!"

"What!?" I said, hardly believing my ears.

Tara then pulled out a golden pouch, and inside was a heart shaped chocolate wrapped in golden foil.

"That girl handed this to me during your show, right after you played 'Write This Down.'"

"Holy sh*t...," I muttered. The synchronicity was almost too much to handle.

At that exact moment, I knew I needed to find space in the book to tell this story. But this part is only the beginning.

SYNCHRONICITY STRIKES AGAIN

Tara and I departed from Sundari the next day to drive to the west side of the island for our three-day shamanic program and plant medicine ceremony. About an hour into our drive, we heard a loud thump and pulled the car over. Sure enough, the Camaro had gotten a flat tire. To make matters worse, there was no spare tire in the trunk. We were both tired and hungry and thought it would be wise to have a snack before trying to deal with the tire situation, so we pulled into the parking lot of a nearby supermarket and went inside. Just as we were about to leave the store, I bumped into Natto again at checkout lane. Very strange, I thought to myself...

I asked him if he had ever read *The Celestine Prophecy* and told him about how when you keep bumping into the same people, especially strangers, it means you were meant to talk to each other. We started making small talk and catching up about how our vacations were going so far. I could tell he was a fun-loving guy just like me who loved music, art, nature, and adventure. We discussed the different areas of Hawaii and he gave me some recommendations.

"I actually live out on the island part of the year and split my time between here and Portland," he said.

"Wow, that's awesome," I said. I then asked him, "Out of curiosity, you wouldn't happen to know where we could find some cannabis out here, do you? Are there any dispensaries?"

"Funny you should ask, man, my buddy I'm going to visit today owns an organic pot and coffee farm out here! I can totally hook you up. Here, take my number."

"Thank you so much, man!" I said as we exchanged numbers. Natto said he'd reach out to me in a day or two.

At this point I was certain I knew why the synchronicity of bumping into him again had occurred. It's usually hard for me to sleep in new places, so I use cannabis when I can as a remedy for insomnia. I was proud of myself for paying attention to the signs and striking up a conversation with him. I was now glad we got the flat tire. It felt like a gift from the universe. Luckily, it was a run-flat tire, designed to still function and not fully deflate when punctured. Our Airbnb host, Joe, was kind enough to patch it for us and fill the tire with his air compressor. We were then able to exchange the car at a service center at no cost and continue our trip.

A LASTING AWARENESS

Later that night, Tara and I arrived at the retreat center for our plant medicine ceremony. We chatted with Jack and ZZ about our travel woes, and Jack commended our ability to stay mindful and grateful throughout the aggravations.

"That attitude will serve you well in life," he said.

The medicine itself was a very interesting experience. It was a tea brewed with several different plants that induced a somewhat hypnogogic, dream-like state of relaxation. While Tara laid down listening to the music with her eyes closed the entire time, I found myself having a stream of continuous thoughts and insights on my life and my book. I was getting all sorts of ideas for ways to promote it and connect with other artists and like-minded individuals.

We had an integration circle at the end of the ceremony to discuss our insights and takeaways, and I realized something extremely profound that had not even crossed my mind during the journey. The person before me shared about her history of sexual abuse and how she is still processing and uncovering new aspects of her trauma sixty years later. Her sharing sparked a valuable insight in me that I had not previously realized. When it was my turn to speak, I discussed how during many of my psychedelic experiences, especially with psilocybin, I feel called to sing. When people talk about having a "bad trip," I remind them there is no such thing as a bad trip—only learning experiences and opportunities for growth. Even when we are reliving a traumatic experience during a plant medicine journey, we are being given the opportunity to reexamine and reinterpret what happened to us.

I realized that the reason singing comforts me and evokes joy during a journey is not just because I am creating harmonious vibrations. By singing, I can consciously direct my journey with sound rather than being at the mercy of whatever thoughts the medicine brings up in my mind. I had become so used to protecting myself against negative experiences that I was not allowing myself to be open to receive the lessons and healing I needed. Instead of letting go, I was holding on and trying to control my journeys and avoid dealing with negative emotions. By wanting to see only the good things, I was not honoring the balance of positive and negative in life.

During my private session with Jack the following day, I became aware of several aspects of my speech that were limiting my growth and awareness of what is possible for me.

"I'm in the middle of trying to record my album of songs for this book I'm writing," I said to Jack.

"Are you trying to do that, or are you doing it?" Jack asked me.

"Well...I guess I haven't really been putting in as much effort as—"

"There's no such thing as trying, Nate," he said. "You either commit to doing something, or you don't."

His words stung with the bitter taste of awareness of my own self-sabotage.

Deep down, I knew I was putting off recording the songs for fear they wouldn't sound good, or that the recordings wouldn't accurately capture my vision.

"What have I been doing this whole time?" I asked myself, apparently out loud, because Jack responded.

"You've been distracting yourself from what you need to do and what your heart is telling you to do."

"Damn," I said. "So, what can I do to overcome those distractions and face the resistance head on?"

Instead of answering, Jack pointed to the folder that was on the table in front of us. I looked down at it.

"Inside that folder is everything you need to know."

When I opened the folder, I found several pages of information on freeing oneself from the traps of the mind. It included a series of mantras called *The 12 Pathways* by Ken Keyes, all of which I have since memorized and recite to myself at different times of the day to help me notice ways I am limiting myself with my thoughts or actions.

Perhaps my favorite of the twelve is, *"I welcome the opportunity, even if painful, that my minute to minute experience offers me to become aware of the addictions I must reprogram to be liberated from my robot-like emotional patterns."*

Later that day, I learned a profound lesson in this exact fashion. After my private session with the shaman, it was Tara's turn, so I took the car and went out to explore.

"Have fun!" I said to Tara. "I'll see you at six-thirty."

I explored the downtown area and stopped into a music shop to play some guitars. At around 5:45 p.m., Natto texted me and asked me to meet him at his hotel. I was so excited and figured I should go there while Tara was in her session so we wouldn't have to drive all the way back downtown afterward. When I arrived, we caught up for a few minutes and I stayed to chat with him and his wife and daughter. I tried to remain mindful of the time, but when I got back to the car, it was already 6:20 p.m. I was only about ten to fifteen minutes away—or so I thought. Everything had been so relaxed during our trip I hadn't even accounted for rush hour traffic.

Tara called me at 6:40 p.m. wondering where I was, and I explained why I was late. Before she hung up the phone, I could hear Jack and ZZ asking where I was.

"He went to pick up weed," I heard Tara say right as the call ended.

Hearing her words aggravated me, but I couldn't figure out why. After all, she was telling the truth. I was mainly annoyed I was still stuck in traffic

By the time I arrived, it was 6:45 p.m., and they were all outside waiting for me.

"What happened?" ZZ asked me. But before I could answer, the conversation shifted to our eco adventure the following day.

"We'll meet here at 10 a.m. and ride together to the nature park," Jack said.

The next day, Jack pulled me aside during our hike to finish our private session from the previous day.

We began discussing the materials in the folder and talking about ways that we as human beings can liberate ourselves from the chains of suffering. We discussed how people have addictions to security, control, and power that keep them from fully relaxing and thriving. I was at a point in my life where I was very proud of everything I'd accomplished. But my commitment to personal excellence and greatness had made me aware of the many ways in which I limit myself, as well as all the things I need to work on. Jack brought up my lateness picking up Tara the night before.

"You told Tara you'd be there. You said, 'I'll see you at six-thirty.' But you weren't because something else was more important to you in that moment. You were so focused on getting the cannabis that you broke your commitment to your partner, who you *say* you love more than anything. But what did you love more in that situation? What did your actions reflect?"

"Dammit," I said, feeling dejected and disappointed in myself. *How could I let her down like that?* I asked myself.

"Now don't beat yourself up over it, Nate. It's in the past. It's a lesson for you now. When you say you're going to do something, follow through. Don't let your addictions blind you from what's most important to you."

I was holding back tears. "Thank you for pointing this out to me, Jack," I said.

I hadn't even considered that I might have an addiction at all. I never thought of my relationship with cannabis as an addiction. It wasn't hindering my ability to be successful and accomplish my goals—or so I thought. My ultimate goal is to give as much love as I can and be there for the people I care about. Sure, I was only fifteen minutes late, but in that moment, I was blinded by my excitement over finally getting to smoke for the first time since leaving home. This realization led me to undertake a lot of deep inner work. I realized how many hours I had spent smoking cannabis instead of finding ways I could better utilize my time. I was burying negative emotions with weed instead of processing those emotions.

"I want to do better," I said. "I want to honor my divine creation and live with purpose."

"The highest form of worship is to enjoy one's life!" Jack said to me. "Focus on creating joy for yourself, and don't look outside for the answers that are already in your heart."

I felt like I was listening to a Nate Jones song or something...

If only I could take my own advice the way I give it, I thought to myself. As we continued our nature hike, I soon realized that regret was not a productive mental state to be in. I started looking around and appreciating the turquoise blue water, the seabirds soaring above me, and the wild goats playing on the nearby rocks. I then looked at the trees and all the plants scattered along the path and began to appreciate them.

Plants are ancient, beautiful, and wise, and they are not the problem. Even the cannabis plant I had questioned my relationship with just moments before is a beautiful and practical medicine when used properly. It wasn't the plant that was the problem, it was my own laziness, excuses, and escape tactics. Once I realized this, I started being nicer to myself and remembering how much cannabis helped me in the wake of my abuse.

I spent many hours writing in my journal and playing guitar after smoking, and all the songs I've written with the help of cannabis deserve to be acknowledged and celebrated. Whenever I was upset and couldn't find the inspiration to play music, this plant was there for me. It helped me let go of limiting beliefs about myself and see my life's journey in a whole new light. If I had not dived so deeply into music, I would not have developed the skills that have since allowed me to write songs and give voice to my heart's true expression.

I made the commitment right then and there to cultivate a deeper respect for the cannabis plant, and to use it only when I truly need it.

My time in Hawaii gave me the inspiration I needed to finish this book in a thoughtful way and make sure I touched upon all the major lessons I've learned in life. Tara and I made the most of the few days we had left, swimming with manta rays at night and hiking to the beautiful Waimea Valley. We also ended up eating the mushroom chocolate together at a place called Pololu Valley, which is by far the most beautiful place I've ever been. The takeaways from the mushroom journey that day helped reinforce the lessons and insights from our trip. Most importantly, I strengthened my commitment to treating my body, mind, and spirit with respect, especially with regard to what I consume.

TIME IS ALL WE HAVE

When you feel like time is dragging on, think about all the times it seems to fly by. What is the difference between the two experiences? A lot of the time, we're checked out, and not living in the moment through focused action. Our goals and objectives for our life at any given moment become an afterthought because of distraction. We can continue to let this happen until our dreams pass us by, or we can lead happy lives by making the most of our time. So, how do we make the most of our time? By spending it doing as many things as we can that make our heart sing!

Whether you're creating personal happiness for yourself through art, music, hobbies, traveling, sports, or meditation, or you're enjoying the happiness that comes from directly helping someone else, you are contributing to the GDH of the entire planet. In case you're wondering, GDH stands for gross domestic happiness, which I also refer to as GDL, or gross domestic love. We all know GDP is not what really matters. So, let's stop pretending it's important!

You are the CEO of your own life, and it's up to you to create a culture of happiness and respect for yourself and your fellow beings. Together, we can focus on the creativity waiting to be explored inside each of us. We can record incredible life-changing music, create artistic masterpieces, write amazing books, and teach each other innovative ways of better caring for ourselves, our fellow beings, and the planet. To do this, we must embrace our art, whatever it may be. We must do the work of cultivating and nourishing the creations blooming inside of us by watering the positive seeds in our mind, and in the process realize our dreams.

Time is all we have.

There's no point in waiting to turn your dreams into reality.

Life is short. Ya gotta make it last!

So... GIVE YOURSELF PERMISSION TO CREATE!

"If you're not the hero of your own novel, then what kind of novel is it? You need to do some heavy editing."
—TERENCE MCKENNA

CONCLUSION

When organizing the themes of the chapters for my editorial review with the publisher, I noticed that what I wrote read quite perfectly as a poem summarizing the message of the book. So, I gave myself permission to create this simple conclusion. Enjoy!

Walk out the door and embark on your life's mission
Create the freedom you seek in life, and don't be afraid to fly
Death is an illusion—our spirit transcends it
Lying within each person is a chemical gateway to a realm of pure love
Practice patience and use compassionate words to keep the darkness at bay
You have the authority to speak your truth
Embrace the changes in life

Keep your options open and pursue what you find meaningful
We are the universe expressing itself in a complex form
Trust your intuition and let it guide your life
Put yourself and your own healing first

Use play to cultivate youthfulness and get in touch with your inner child

Magic is real, and we are all magicians

Slow down and enjoy life

What everyone is looking for is already inside of us

One day is all that it takes to change your life

Be okay with not having all the answers

Your actions lead to your circumstances in life—you can't blame others

Reflection helps you gain perspective on your past and future dreams

The love that is meant for you will find you when the time is right

Go out into nature to release your inner peace and show the world what you discover

Have compassion for all beings and be accountable for how your actions affect others

Existence is bliss when we cultivate the energy of mindfulness

Don't take yourself too seriously, trust the intelligence of our planet

There is more of you under the surface than what is visible

Acknowledge your growth and honor the many different layers of yourself

Life is short, make it last and live in the moment

Now go create!

HONORABLE MENTION QUOTES

———

The following are a list of quotes from some of my spiritual mentors that deeply resonate with me, but that I could not find space for in the book. I hope you enjoy these statements, and if any in particular resonate with you, I highly encourage you to research the author.

"Life is like music for its own sake. We are living in an eternal now, and when we listen to music, we are not listening to the past, we are not listening to the future, we are listening to an expanded present."

—ALAN WATTS

"The most precious gift we can offer anyone is our attention. When mindfulness embraces those we love, they will bloom like flowers."

—THICH NHAT HANH.

"In any moment, you have a choice that either leads you closer to your spirit, or further away from it."

—THICH NHAT HANH

"Attachment to view is the greatest impediment to the spiritual path."

—THICH NHAT HANH

"Culture is the effort to hold back the mystery and replace it with a mythology."

—TERENCE MCKENNA

"We have to create culture, don't watch TV, don't read magazines, don't even listen to NPR. Create your own roadshow. The nexus of space and time where you are now is the most immediate sector of your universe, and if you're worrying about Michael Jackson or Bill Clinton or somebody else, then you are disempowered, you're giving it all away to icons, icons which are maintained by an electronic media so that you want to dress like X or have lips like Y. This is shit-brained, this kind of thinking. That is all cultural diversion, and what is real is you and your friends and your associations, your highs, your orgasms, your hopes, your plans, your fears. We are told 'no,' we're unimportant, we're peripheral. 'Get a degree, get a job, get a this, get a that.' Then you're a player, but you don't want to even play in that game. You want to reclaim your mind and get it out of the hands of the cultural engineers who want

to turn you into a half-baked moron consuming all this trash that's being manufactured out of the bones of a dying world."

—TERENCE MCKENNA

Referring to the internet: "Some kind of dialogue is now going on between individual human beings and the sum total of human knowledge and nothing can stop it."

—TERENCE MCKENNA

"Half the time you think you're thinking, you're actually listening."

—TERENCE MCKENNA

"If you had known me when I was nineteen years old, I was into Jean-Paul Sartre, Albert Camus, Marxism, Freud... I was a jerk! And I came down from it (DMT) and I said 'I can't believe it!' That was all I could say for twenty minutes. And I said, you know, I gotta go back to square one, all these people I dismissed, all these people who say the Universe is made of levels, who say there are disincarnate intelligences, who say that death is not simply the yawning grave, I had dismissed all those people as crybabies and sob sisters."

—TERENCE MCKENNA

"The artist's task is to save the soul of mankind. Anything less is a dithering while Rome burns. If artists cannot find the way, then the way cannot be found."

—TERENCE MCKENNA

ACKNOWLEDGMENTS

Adam J Drici
Alex Procaccini
Alexander J Sotis
Alexander Santomarco
Amanda Russo
Amanda Way
Anand Sukhadia
Andrea Canale
Andreas Altenburg
Andrew Greenbaum
Andrew Penk
Andrew Vu
Armida Martinez
Axios Papaflessas
Brendan Barbato
Brian Bouchard
Bruce Hamlin
Bruce Keiser
Casey Miller
Chelsea St Jacques
Jed and Danielle Fluehr

Crystal Psotta
Cynthia and Ray Erickson
Daniel Roberts
Daniel Torres
Diana Anderson
Deanna Moretti
Deborah Radcliff
Debra Pittman
Derek Januszewski
Eric Koester
Eric Vaught
Freddy Larrosa
Gail and Jeff Poliquin
Gary Luiz
Gilaad Amir
Hal Corcoran
Hannah McGuirl
Hayley McGuirl
Hillis Pugh
Jaime Kilday
Jake Therien

James Nealy
James Rajewski
Jane and Nate Albro
Janet and Lino Rego
Jason Falls
Jennifer Gonsalves
Jennifer Peavey
Jennifer Shepherd
Jessica Lee Alton
Joe Rivera
John Byrne
John Ferris
John Lacki
Jonathan Mitchell
Kate Burnes
Kathleen Carty
Kayla Aguiar
Kerri Micheletti
Kerry Cudmore
Kevin Burgess
Kevin Price
Kevin Shepherd
Kimberly Madden
Lani Park
Laurin Cabralissa
LeeAnn Cagnina
Leo Beaudet
Lorie Gilligan
Loury Azucena
Marisa Pfohl
Mark Flynn
Mark Jones

Marqui Williams
Mary Palombo
Melissa Impett
Nate Jones
Nathan Corey
Nicholas S Jones
Olivia Rose
Patricia Alton
Patricia and Michael Procaccini
Patricia Vaillancourt
Patrick T Luiz
Rachel Arthur
Randi Sherman
Raymond Erickson Jr.
Rebecca Lawton
Bill and Cinthia Reppe
Robert Paternostro Jr.
Robert Walker Cohen
Robin Berghorn
Ryan Farin
Sabrina Chapman
Sheena Sullivan
Siobhan Reynolds
Starr Truthbringer
Stephen Bell
Steve Cravin
Steve Atlas
Stevie Downie Jr.
Tara Lee Conner
Teresa A Marcolivio
Tom and Kathy Palombo

Thomas Malitsky
Wendy Negron
Wyatt Burg
Zaida Raquel Garcia

REFERENCES

———

CHAPTER 5

Strassman, Rick. *DMT: The Spirit Molecule: A Doctor's Revolutionary Research into the Biology of Near-Death and Mystical Experiences*. Rochester, Vt. Park Street Press. 2001.

CHAPTER 8

Levitin, Daniel J. *This Is Your Brain on Music the Science of a Human Obsession*. Paw Prints. 2008.

CHAPTER 9

Sincero, Jen. *You Are a Badass at Making Money: Master the Mindset of Wealth*. John Murray Learning. 2018.

CHAPTER 15

"Merriam-Webster Dictionary." Merriam-Webster.com. 2021. https://www.merriam-webster.com/dictionary/spell#:~:text-t=1a%20%3A%20a%20spoken%20word. 2021.

CHAPTER 27

Keyes, Ken. *Handbook to Higher Consciousness.* Guernsey The Guernsey Press Co. Ltd. 1997.

9 781637 303566